Cracking

Charles Simonds and
Lucy R. Lippard

VERLAG DER BUCHHANDLUNG
WALTHER KÖNIG, KÖLN

Cracking

Cracking

From this cave. Over this hill. Through this valley. The people came this way. When did they come? Then. When do they come? Now. These two. One looking east and the other west. One wanting to dig not deep enough. The other wanting to dig too deep.

March 19: My first impression was of a dusty distant untouched space. Red, a burning, sterile red, rejecting green. The land rolling here, twisted there into a cone or mound, pressed here into itself leaving a gaping aperture, a cracked dry lakebed, traces of geometry, or rising there into a mountain range that never seems near. As I walked with my eyes, inwards, a delicate dusting of green became apparent—more like moss than grass, not covering the red mounds and flats but mottling them, as passing clouds will shadow the land on a sunny day. Is it so far away, or so close—that it demands a special focus, a foreign lens?

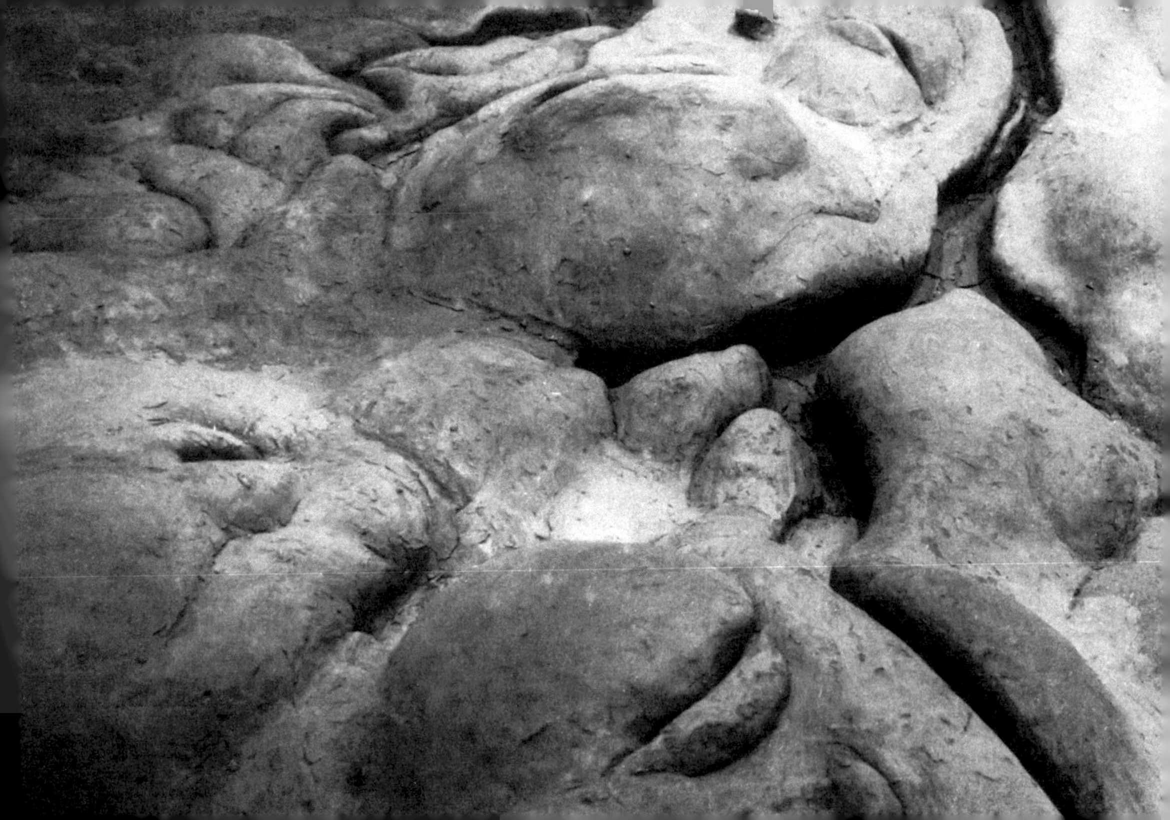

Try to remember that most of the evidence has vanished. All we will find is the accidentally durable. We are working with bare bones. Working in a void. It is our responsibility never to overstep the facts.

On the contrary. Our responsibility is to breathe life into the facts, to flesh the bones, to fit the shards together, constantly to transcend the facts, expand the remains with our own lives. But I don't know this, yet.

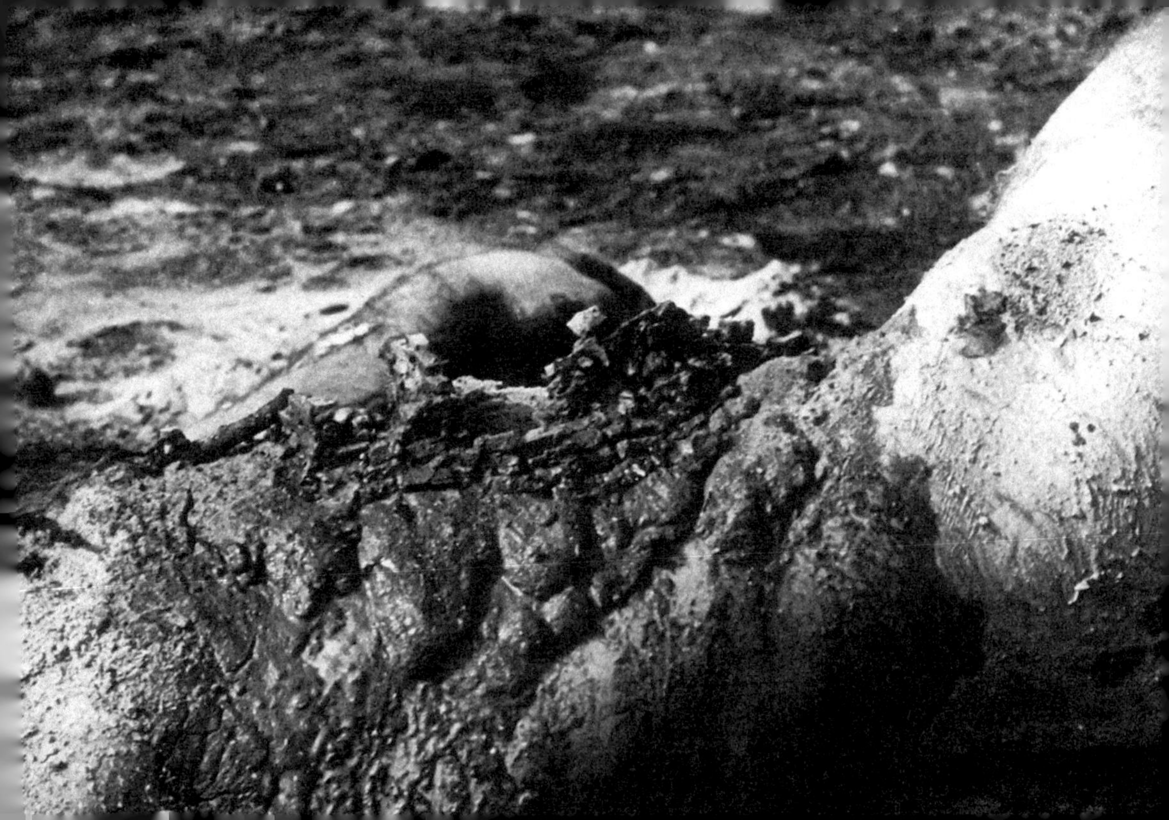

March 20: I am accused of being a colonist. Archeology should be the opposite of colonization. It should be the process of reseeding, restoring to life the myths and values of a lost society, rather than of smothering them with one's own civilization. But do we ever escape our own? X sees the past as childish and underdeveloped in comparison to current "advances". I see the past as a means of understanding why our society is *not* progressing. Perhaps the truth lies in the interstices but X is embarrassed by speculation and prefers to look the other way when I poke my finger into crevices. Instead of making mysteries mundane, instead of using this limitation to reinforce our own severely limited mythology, shouldn't we use it to open things up? To stimulate our imaginations about the future?

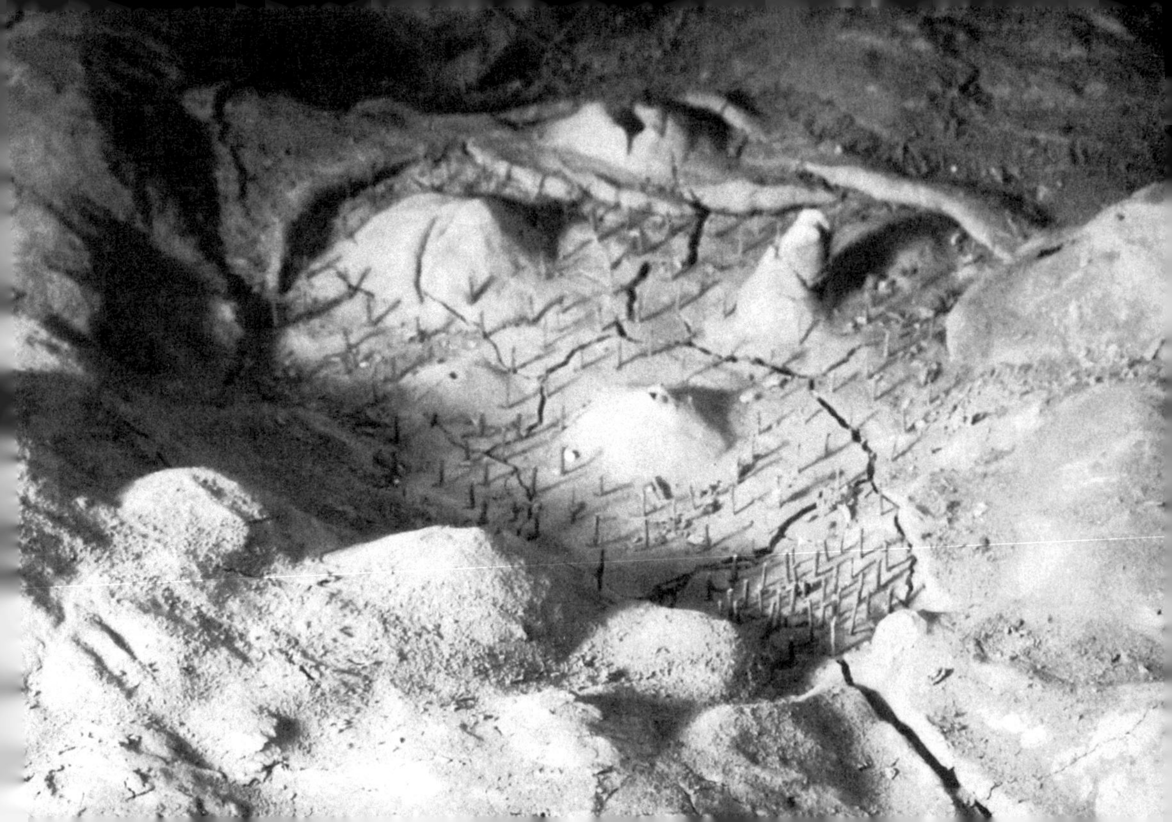

It is a strangely lifeless landscape, except for the butterflies. They come in swarms at dusk—blue and violet and white and jade—all the cool colors forgotten here. They seem to be sucking the life from the hot little flowers that straggle from cracks in the rocks and line the sandy ditches. Yet the flowers, closing at the end of the day just when they might attract some moisture, will open up again at the touch of a butterfly's wings and stay open after contact, so they do indeed catch some dew. Those unvisited wilt visibly as the sun plunges behind the mountain. The butterflies live in the caves, those peaked slits in the rock where people once lived too. The last thing we see on a moonless night is a thin ghostly trail disappearing into the darkest reaches.

There are no snakes here.

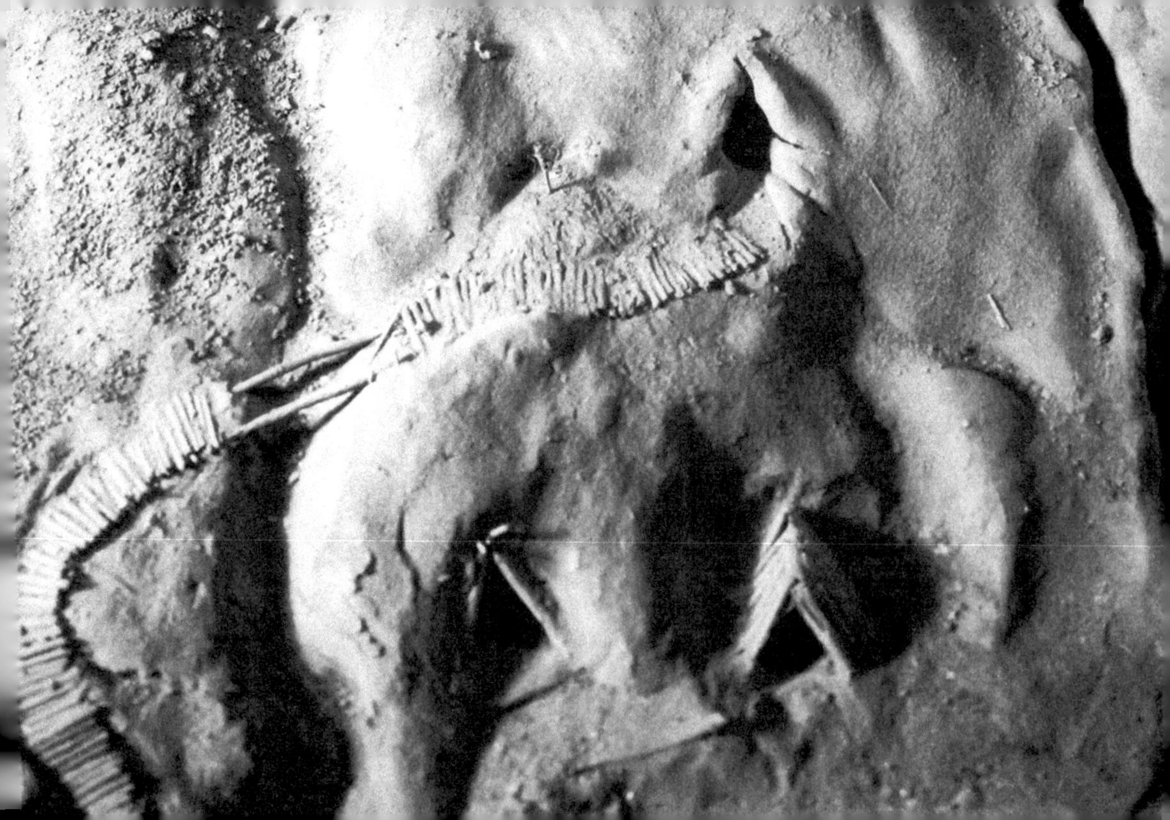

March 21: The surveys are completed, the long long walks over every inch of this harsh but intimate terrain sadly come to an end. Today we begin to dig, halting for occasional dust storms. The climate must once have been very different, for we have found a layer of lush vegetation, still damp, apparently picked and used as a layer in the foundations of whatever structure this is we have found—for symbolic rather than for functional reasons?

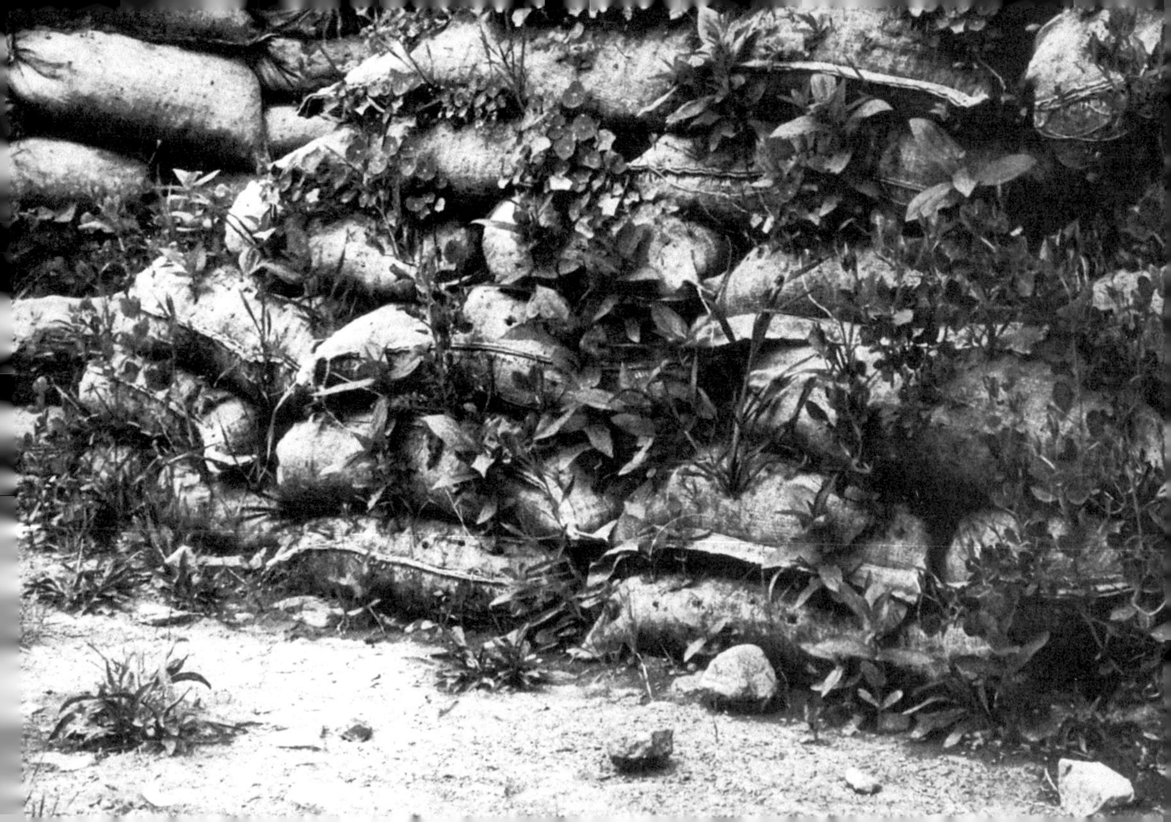

Some sort of ritual seems to have taken place here. Look, the ground is turned and tossed and trodden as though dances had been danced on the wet earth. And that avenue—there—leading into the hill ...

Nonsense. That is only the path to the well. And your "dance floor"—why, that is where they threshed their wheat. And that structure—a barracks, no doubt.

A home, at least.

The earthworks are obviously animal pounds.

Generations of labor, over a million man-hours to build an animal pound? Where were the animals kept in the meantime?

That vegetation is garbage. The tower is part of a system of military defenses.

A one-sided watchtower with no view to the other side? Garbage? Those twisted strands radiating from a central knot? No! You're depriving them of their real lives.

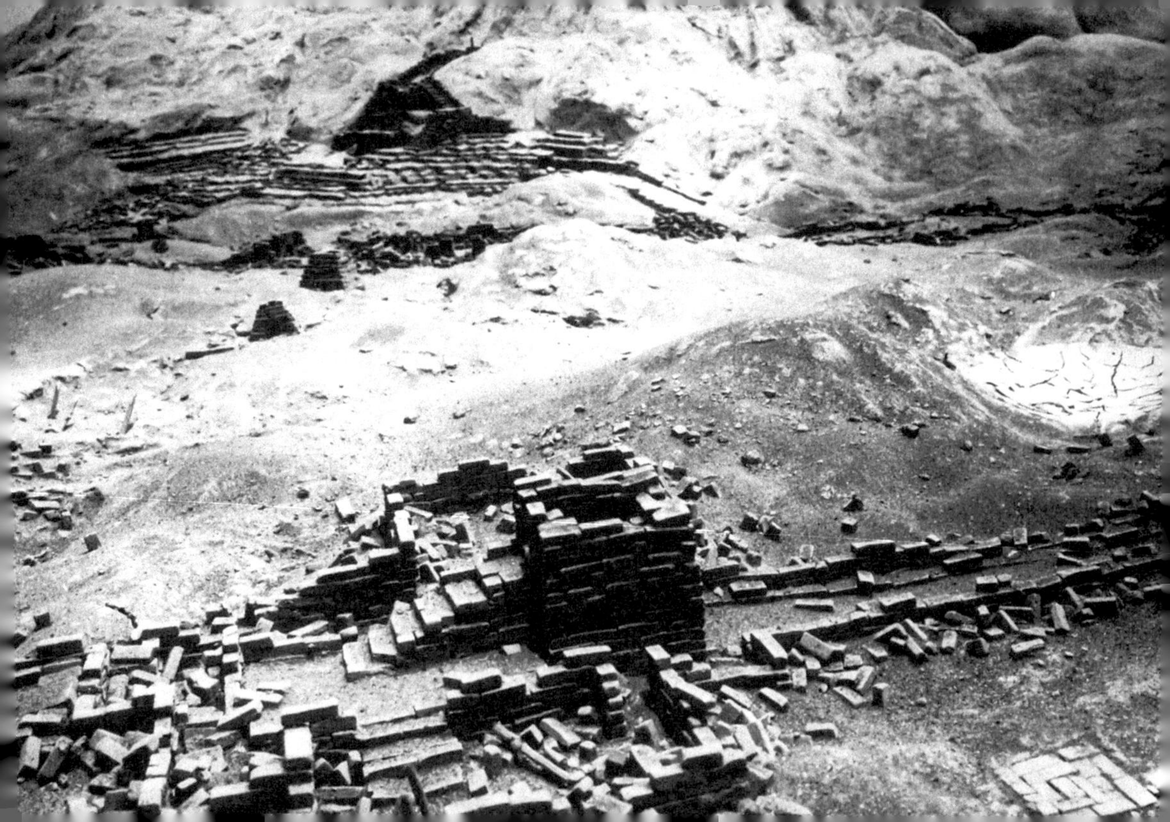

March 22: The paths, the touches begin to emerge. This is not a barren and unloved landscape but a collaboration with roots deeper in the past than we dare consider. A collaboration born of itself and continuing today. A collaboration of which I am suddenly a part. People have risen from, been nurtured by, worshipped, gradually and respectfully altered every inch of these red contours. Who? What people? Why?
It must be spring. More light is shed on our labor. I hear drumming underground and we make premature contact with the green shoots among the buried bricks.

March 25: X insists that it is a road we have found, but he cannot explain the double-tiered structure, the enclosures—in short, the *rooms* that form the road.

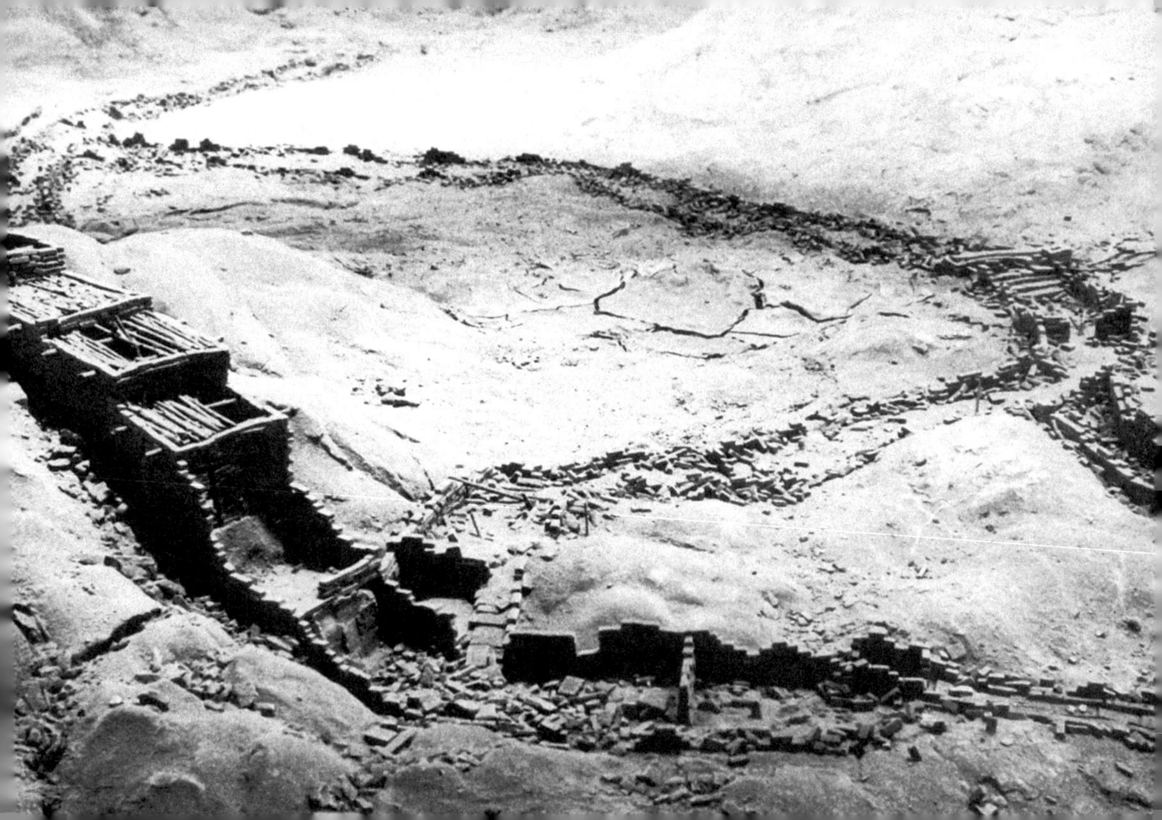

March 26: Today our "road dwelling" branched off to the east and west after a sharp curve in its direct if serpentine meander. Here and there alongside, inexplicable changes occur in the landscape—groups of cairns, notched hills and curious eroded cones with cleft summits, some surrounded by stone circles, others by a paved triangular court. X continues to expect a "palace" at the end of this "royal road". He says the partitioned areas were market stalls, I very much doubt this. We are being led on a journey across the land and it is not a hierarchal journey, not a journey up, but out.

March 28: Last night, walking in the moonlight between the crumbling walls we have disinterred, I had the most extraordinary sense of an attempted communication. Like the beginnings of a dream lying in a dense mist. I can describe nothing at all about this feeling. The barriers lie in my own mind. Something of great value is hidden here.

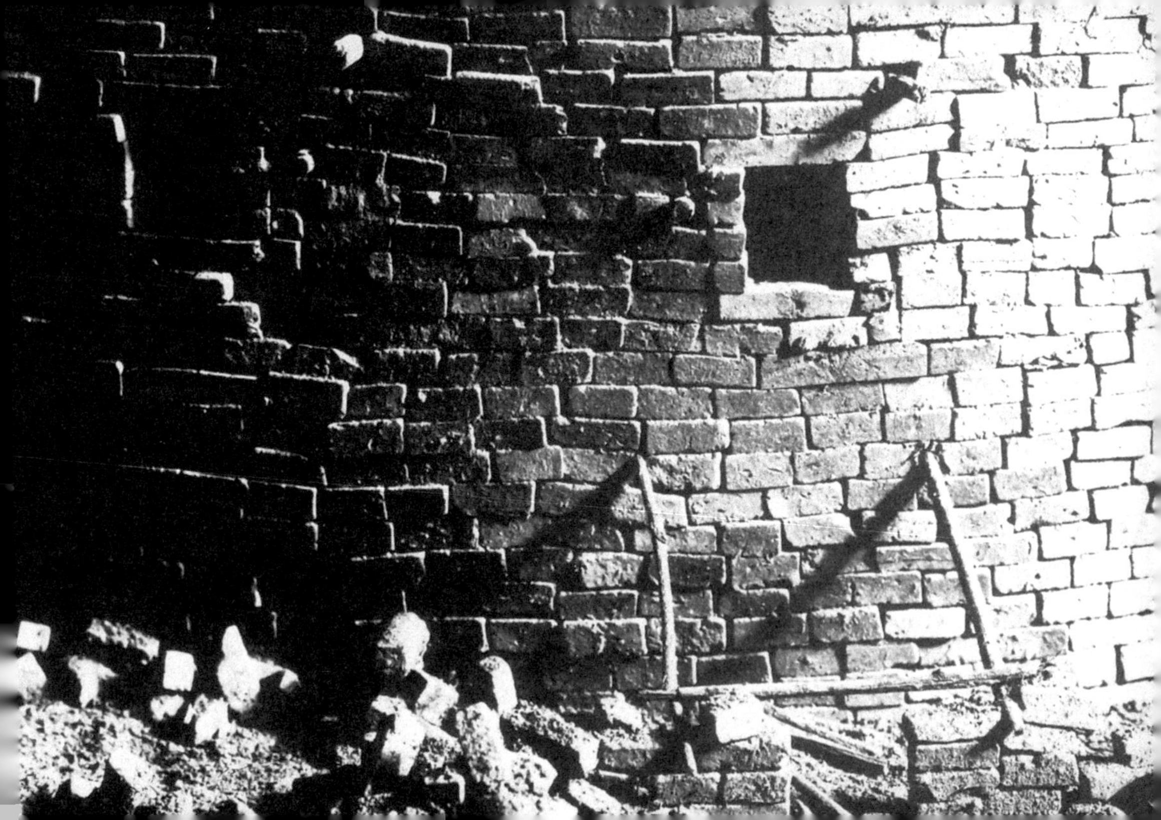

March 31: The east branch has simply stopped. Or rather it has descended into the earth near three small truncated ziggurats. Under them we found charcoal deposits and a curious collection of shards with brief inscriptions. They are not something broken; they are parts that have yet to come together. One is triangular in form, the picture running off the apex. Another, found beneath the largest tower, is almost square, and blank. Another, circular, has a single pictograph—a seedlike oval shape— at its center. Others are tiny facets, sharp-edged commas and exclamations, polygons with corners missing, portraits, tendrils, spirals, overlaid circles, bricks with which to build a vocabulary. Around the ziggurats is a field of upright snakes—I mean stakes—buried deep in the ground. These appear as the dwelling-road disappears. We return to the fork tomorrow to begin work on the west branch.

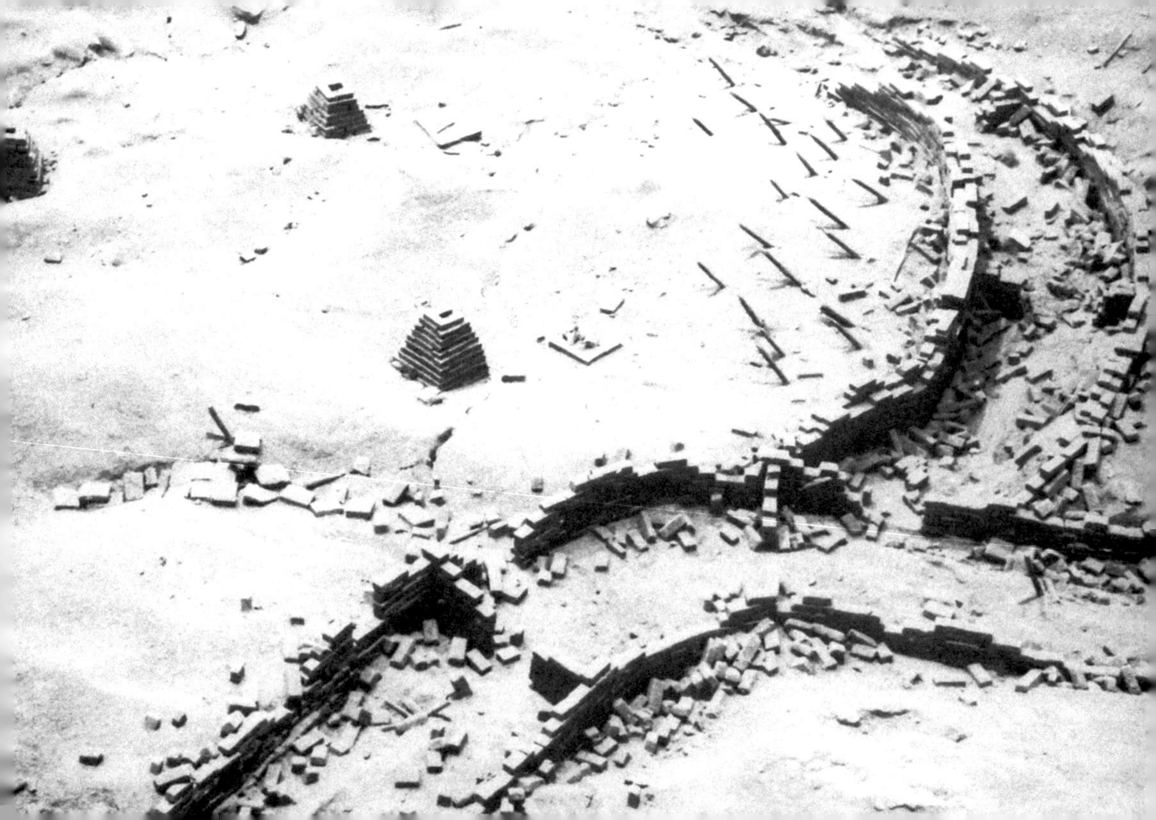

April 14: I dreamt I was walking along a road paved with bricks. I started out alone and then was joined by shadowy figures whom I recognized as my family. After what seemed a very long time, months, perhaps, or even years we saw another small group coming across from the mountain and they joined us. The dream continued like this for what seemed an interminable duration. Nothing happened. We passed mounds and curling hilltops and towers and courtyards and ruins like exaggerated, almost nightmarish versions of the landforms in this place. Individuals and groups of individuals joined the procession, fell away from it or grouped differently so that we were a constantly changing number of units flowing forwards and at times branching out, like cells in some unknown organism. Our movements seemed predetermined but in no way unnatural. I was not aware of myself except as a part of this whole. This whole, which surrounded me with warm flesh, had some tale to tell. But either I was not told or I cannot remember what the message was.

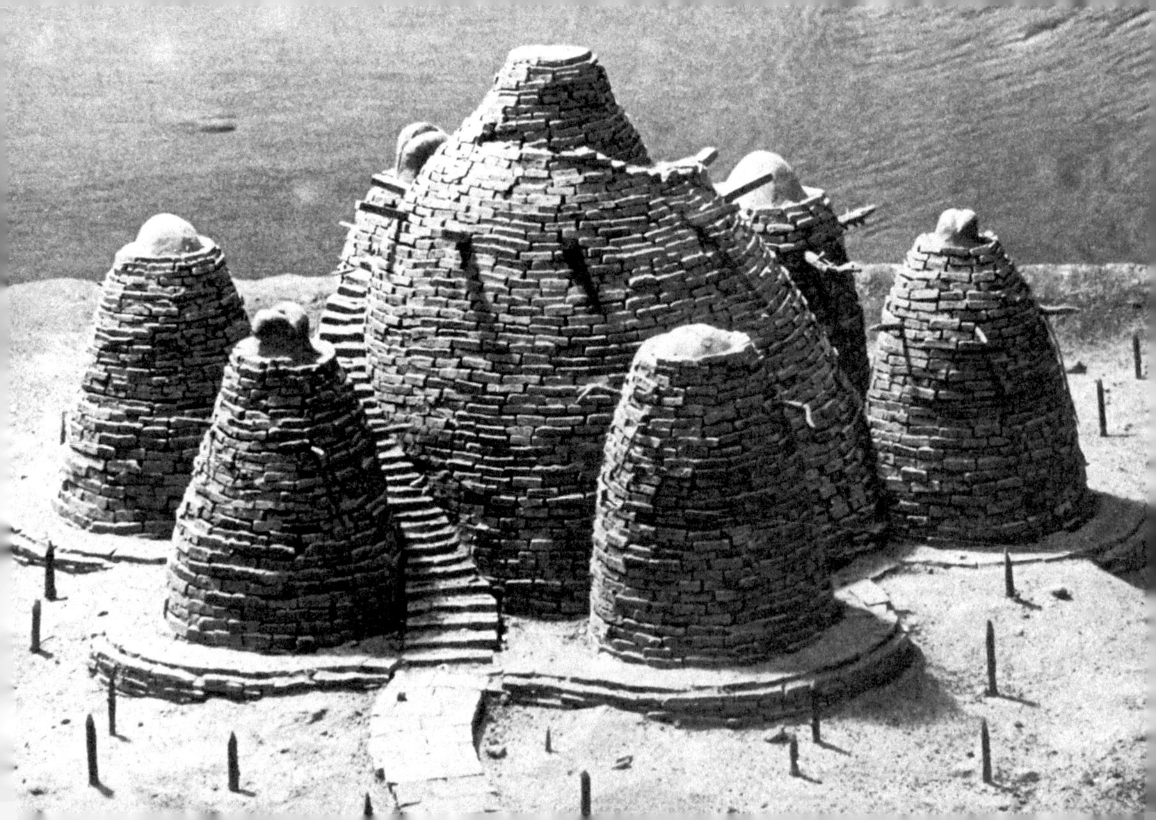

April 18: Some of these endless undulating hills are human-made. Why in such hilly country construct more hills?
There is a haunting aura of timelessness about this place. And at the same time an almost frantic sense of compression. Our excavations do not offer the kind of strata we expected. It is as though eons have been pressed into years, ontogeny and phylogeny mingled.
Would that explain this need to thrust new, straight lines through gentler ruins of the past which later overgrew the angles and interred the future? Would that explain this passion for building, abandoning, re-inhabiting, as though they were trying to repeat all known natural forms in their life span? Oh! The agony of being unable to communicate, of sensing without knowing. I sit here sifting the red dust through my fingers and blowing it across my page. We have turned nature into cliches, fairy tales, and finally a Great Mystery so that by now we see better with instruments and camera lenses than we do with our own bodies.

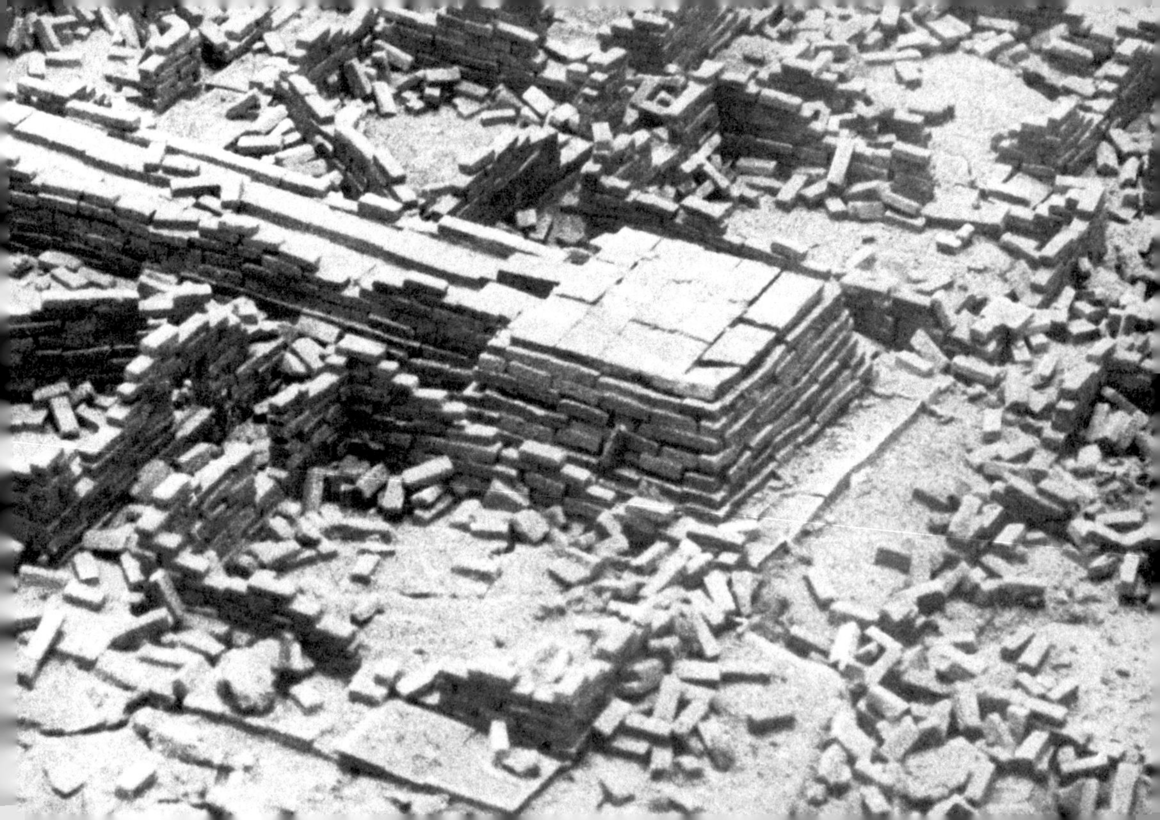

April 21: Wandering today on one of our more random than intended ways toward camp among the foothills of the mountain, just above, but invisible from the last of the straight towered road, we glimpsed the entrance to a natural cavern. Glimpsed it only, as it is hidden behind two dome-shaped hills. The faintest traces of a path paved with water- rounded stones led up the slope. We turned away.

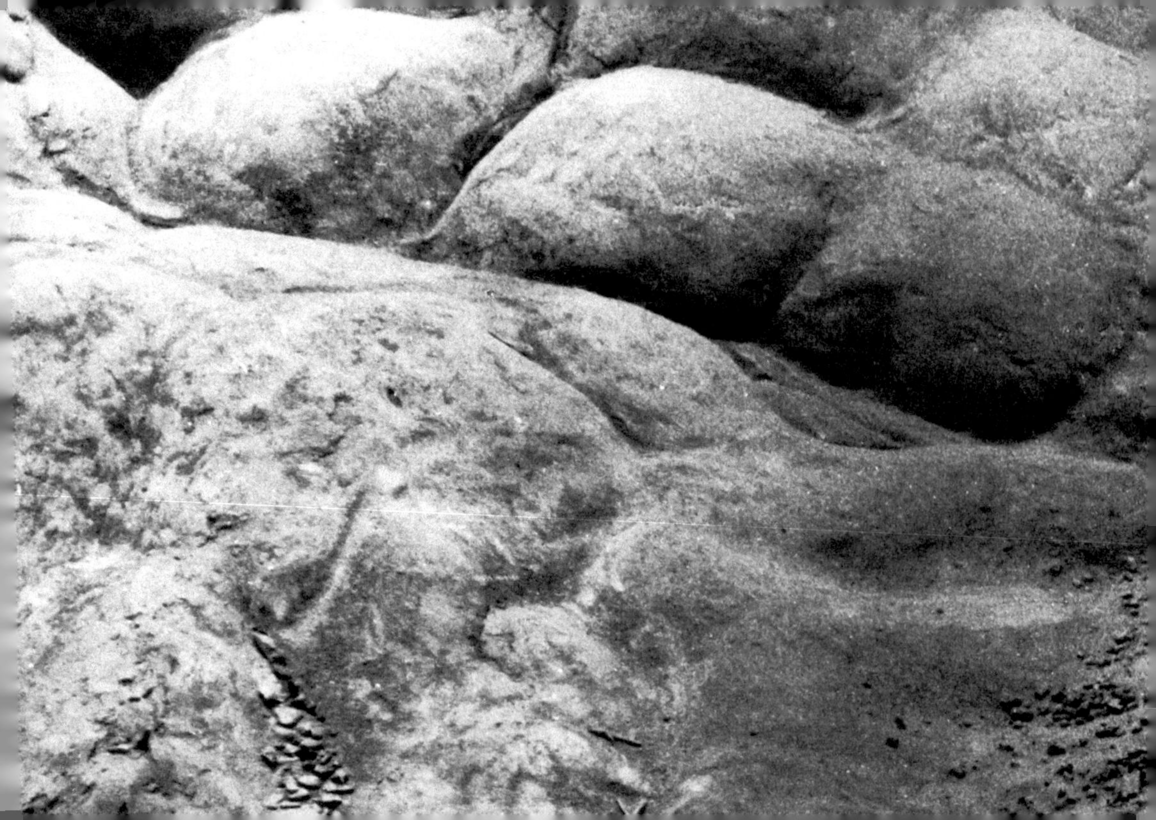

April 27: Last night I dreamt I was standing in the quarry below the mountain. As I watched, the granite blocks above separated, and in the crevasses appeared hundreds of tiny flatroofed houses and a networks of paths leading among the cliffs to circular enclosures and brick-domed hills and strange tumescent knolls and orchards of dead trees. Then I was walking on those paths. I came to the arched mouth of a cave that seemed to lead inside the mountain. Without fear, I entered and followed, joining a long procession—that same body now so persistently invading all my dreams. Eventually the tunnel opened out into a huge bowl-shaped valley dotted by fires through which the procession walked and leapt and cavorted. No one was burned. Each fire was reflected in a rippling blue-green sky, as though we danced underwater, or between two layers of an element that was neither earth nor air nor water but all three combined.

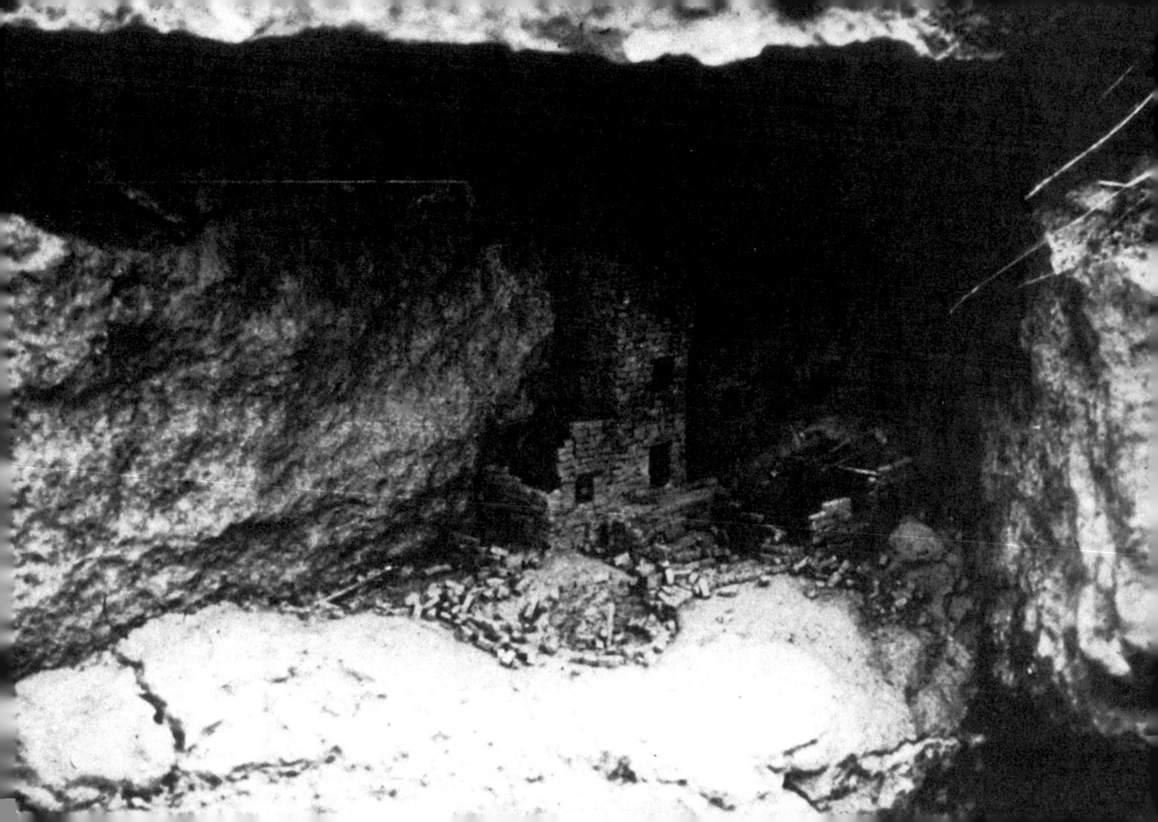

The invisible energies of the universe came together in a coil and formed a serpent, a spiral from which the waters burst. Then the serpent stretched full length, yearning for the opposite directions, and the horizons were born. Then it thrust the firm fat pulsing part of itself into the warm wet open part of itself and the cycles began. Our god is a goddess and our goddess is a god. The first offspring was the earth mother. Seething in eagerness, she pushed up from under her boundaryless mass of mud a brown man, her son and her lover, who, like his mother, had bones of rock and flesh of soil and blood of streams and hair of growing things. In the ecstasy of birth, which was also their first mating, the son tossed, thrashed, squirmed and writhed with the great soft body of his mother. Monuments to this great event remain in all the hills and caves and valleys where we live today.

What? Who's there? Come back! Why is this not a dream?

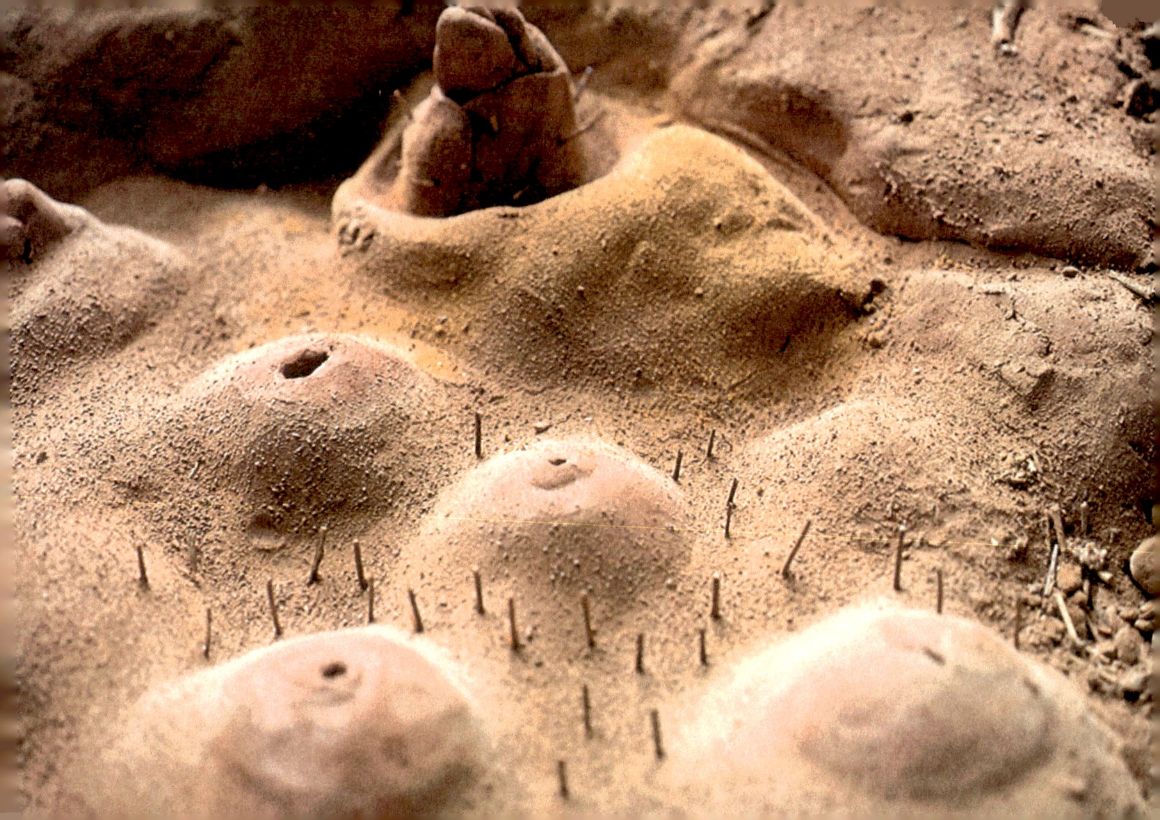

May 1: We have discovered a field of apparently ritual cairns—coneshaped, finely constructed of stone like the walls of the buildings. They are perched on a ledge over the riverbed near the ravine where the great falls was. Some are immense and some are only a few inches high. X says the disparity in size has to do with the importance of the people buried there. The tall ones are for kings and the tiny ones for women and children. The fact we have found no burials he attributes to grave robbers and high acid content of the soil.
I wonder. Couldn't they be a tribute to the equality of great and small? A reminder of how time erodes the greatest erections and how, simultaneously, the tiniest seeds are growing?
Neither of us has mentioned the hole, the cavern in the mountain. We might as well not have seen it.

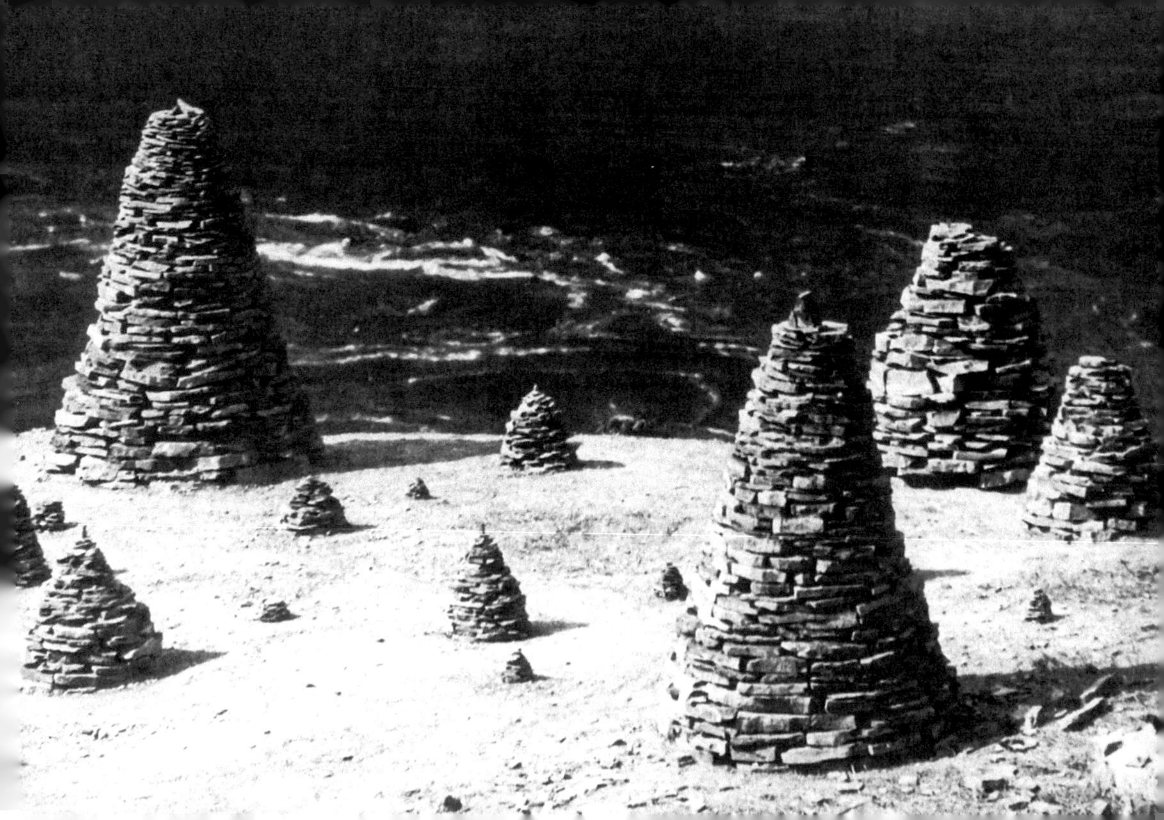

There is no right size here. I seem to be twins. I shrink and stretch as we continue working. Sometimes smallness is intimacy, enterable and sometimes it is threatening in its insistent distance. Inside and outside are states of mind. Small places can be discovered. Large places impose themselves. Who are we to say large and small? To judge the scale of another culture or even the life or view of another person? Where we come from people prefer to feel large. I am trying to learn to be small here.

May 11: There is a strangely sexual aspect to this work. We kneel all day like children on the beach, with our faces close to our excavations, caressing them with tiny instruments. The minutiae, the tedium of tininess. The slow brushing away of veils of dust. The tense, unbearably drawn-out exploration of the unknown, the coming climax of the find.

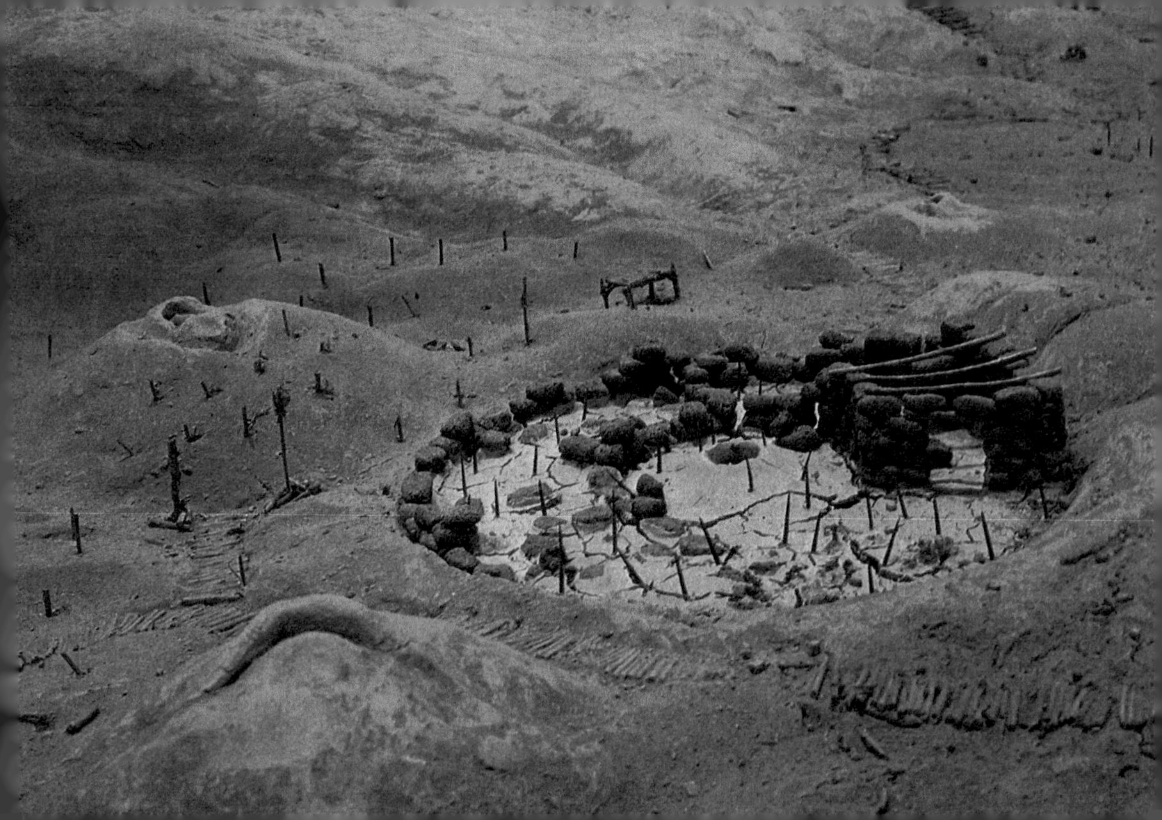

May 30: It is difficult to reconcile the sharp-edged triangular pavements with the curving paths of the "older" landscapes on which they are superimposed. I have to agree with X that the rectangular ramps and towers had some other than ceremonial function. They look very business-like, even menacing. The same psyche surely produced the armored mounds, bristling with protrusions, yet the data suggests that they co-existed with the soft, meandering forms. Two warring cults? Cliffdwellers and herder-farmers? Or factions of the same? Invaders? Warriors, philosophers or scientists? Merchant-artists or astronomer priests? Class struggle? Why did they hide from the people the sacred places and the secrets of their past? What was imprisoned in those strange towers with the channeled tops? What slid down those ramps, flowed through those gutters? Water? Molten metal? Blood?

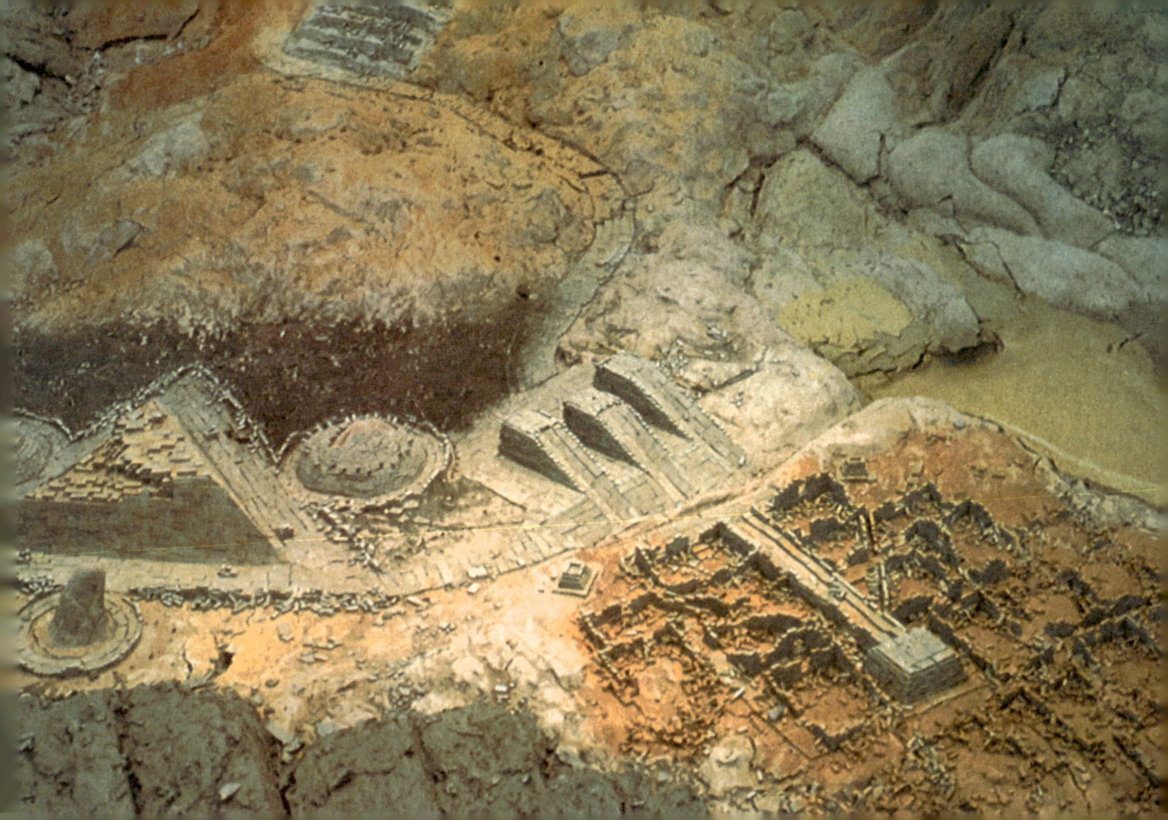

June 21: It must be summer. The hot wind would have shifted the grasses and creatures would have been busy beneath the leaves.

I dreamed a brown man giving birth in pink and yellow mountains farther away than he. I dreamed a brown man giving birth on a rock in the sea and the waves leapt behind him as he touched his progeny. I dreamed a brown man giving birth by a white river hiding its filth. I dreamed a brown man giving birth among the stone cones over the whirlpool. I dreamed a brown man giving birth in the deep pine woods and his children were not mine.

X has refused to include in our reports my speculations concerning the uses of the ritual places.

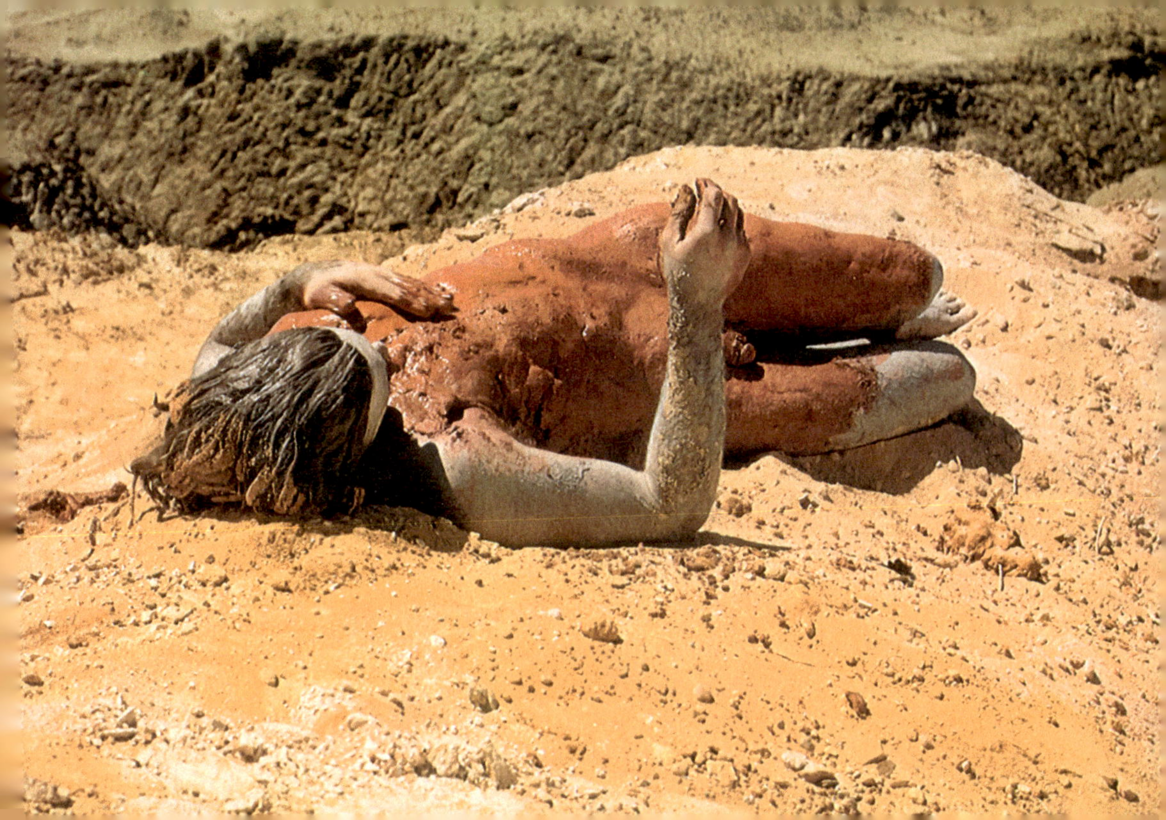

July 2: How to explain the discrepancy in the size of the building units? From grains of sand to tiny bricks to massive five-ton blocks of granite, they are employed interchangeably. What foreign sense of scale pervades this place? When we photograph the ruins, involuntary metamorphoses respond. Structures that are perceptually large shrink and rest daintily in the landscape when recalled in two dimensions, while modest cones and domes and stake forests, a single brick, can swell to intimidating statures. Our measures—the best that modern technology has to offer—seem to follow some other law than that by which they were manufactured, and when introduced for scientific scale they play tricks on the lens and the viewer. A maddening place. Where nothing is the same from day to day and nothing ever changes. It is any wonder we become disoriented, embittered, enraptured?

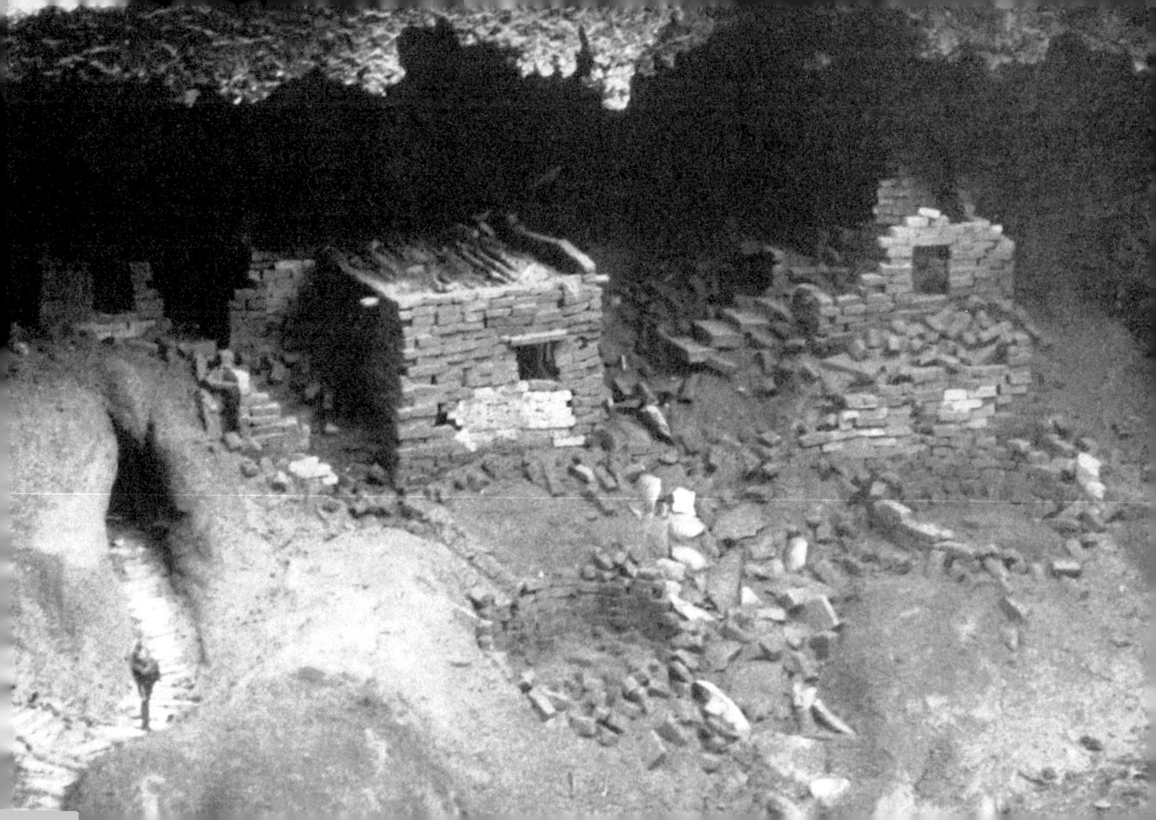

July 13: On the straight road today from the fire towers to the circle city we did not look to our left. X walked ahead. I looked and saw nothing. Perhaps the mouth of the cavern is hidden again behind the two round hills. But I noticed for the first time a stream of water cutting a new channel in the bald eroded earth between them. I made a ball of the mud and rolled it between my palms until it was a long thin coil, warm from my flesh.

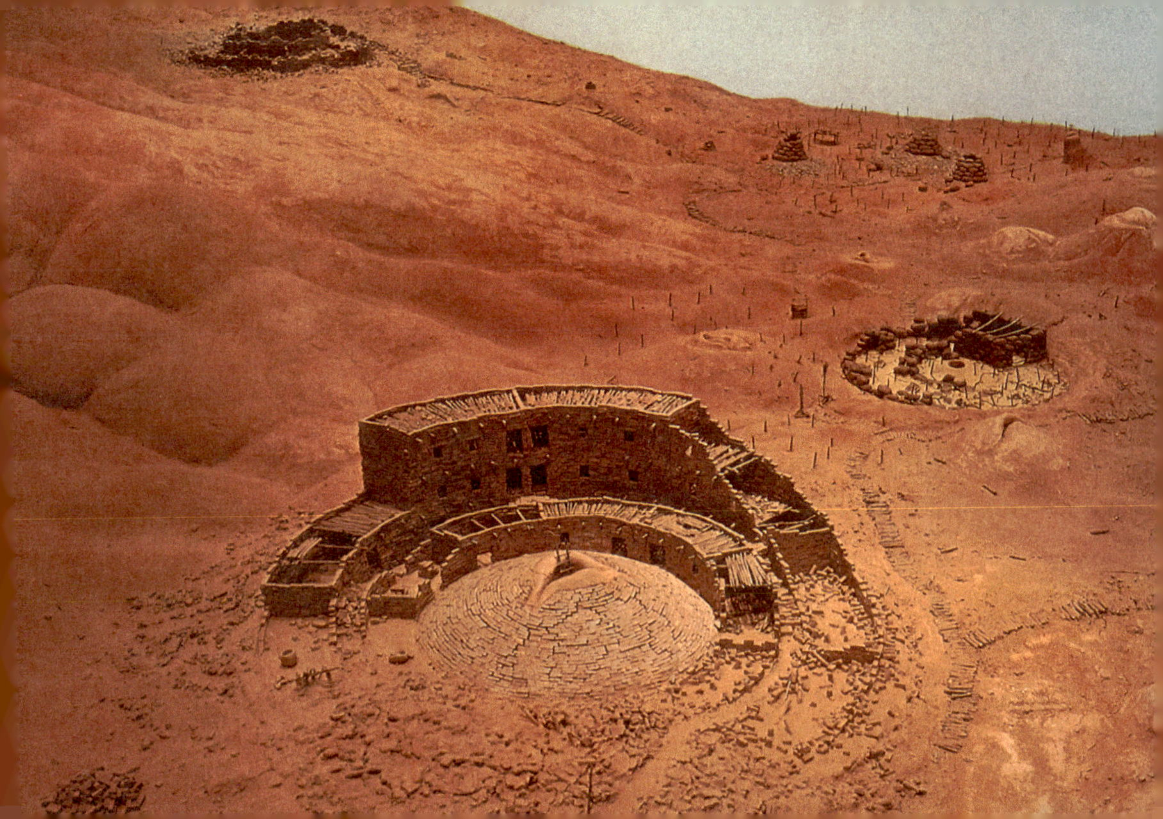

July 19: No dreams for a week now. I feel cut off, abandoned. I cannot find the key to their movements. And movement is the key to their culture.
But not the placid and predictable nomadism X is trying to impose on all this contradictory evidence. The patterns of their travel, reflected in their architecture and their sculptured landscape, are tied to some greater design that is hidden from us. Does that pattern recapitulate social decay in the life of the individual? All journeys are circular. They knew this. So their various migrations—up, down, across, in a line, in a spiral, in concentric circles, in a maze, in the hodgepodge of a city more like ours, in a ritual garden—all took place within a greater circle whose periphery is transformative, boundary without boundaries. Is that it? Your answers are so faint, so bound in layers too.

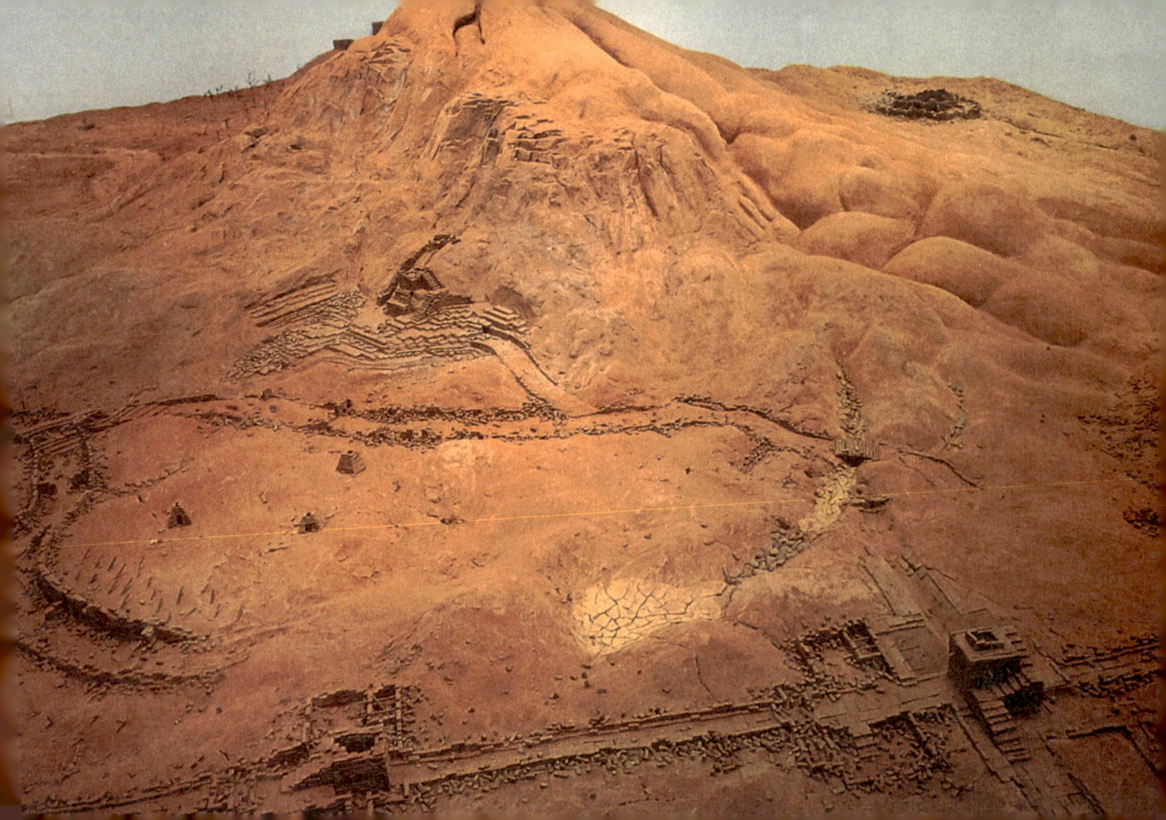

Did the people move slowly into the land? Living first in its natural orifices, worshipping the body as it lay?
Then more self-consciously did they pay homage from huts still camouflaged beginning to help meanings emerge from earthly forms?
Did the "fast life" replace the "slow life" after the cataclysm?
After the earthquakes, after the geysers blew holes through the breasts of the land?
Did it stem from a desire to live the people's entire history every year?
To overlay the growth cycle and double up on time?
Did it end because the snakes and their travelling followers disappeared and eventually the pace became so fast it merged again into original chaos?

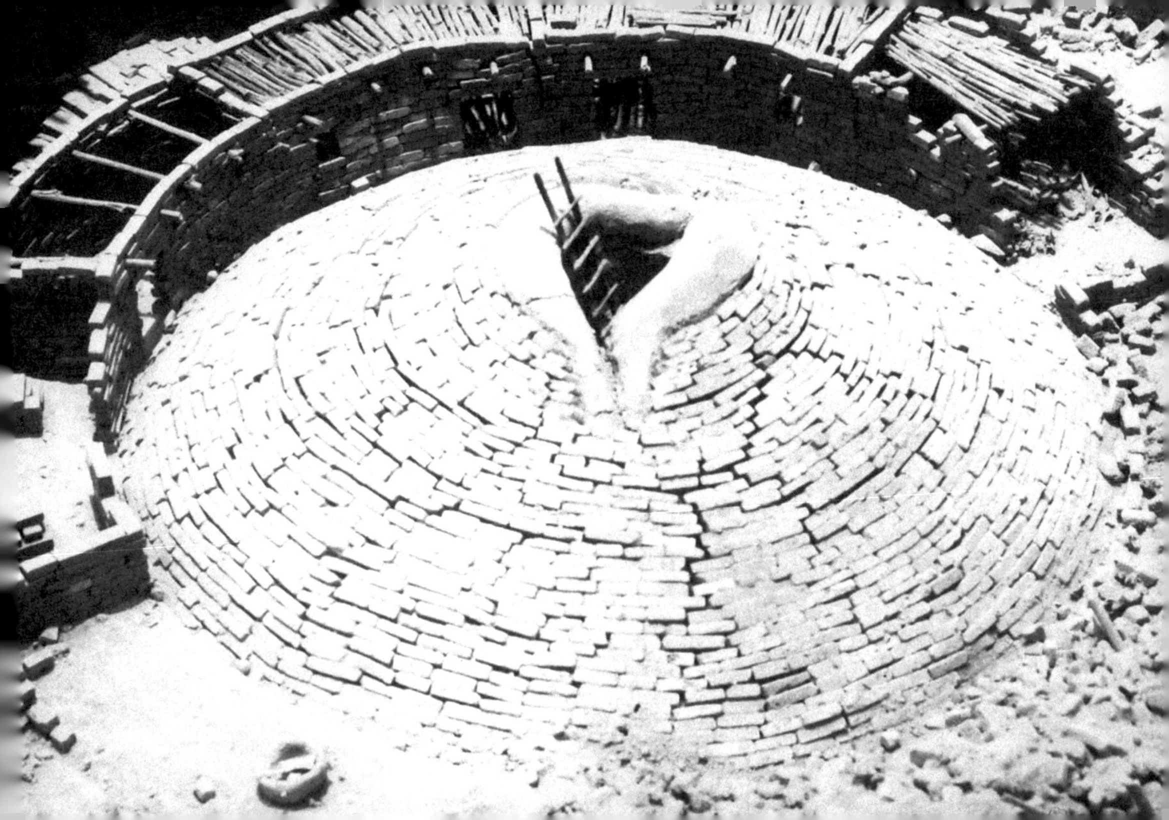

July 23: X says I am obsessed. That it is unbecoming and unprofessional. But he himself keeps worrying over the fact that there are no snakes in this very suitable climate. Once there were tiny lizards, because we have found them in what he insists on calling the "root cellar" at the center of the round city; they are circled back into themselves, swallowing their tails. X thinks his musings about snakes, unlike mine, are harmless, unconnected with our work. It seems his hobby is herpetology. I didn't know that.

August 1: Today, at last, under anxious circumstances, we came upon the first burial. But is it a burial? We found the bones in a stratum so close to the surface that it seems they must not have been buried at all, but simply strewn across the earth. Initially we thought they were scattered at random but then we became aware that they were distributed in a pattern, the nature of which was soon revealed. Where we dug first we found bones, both human and animal— *but only leg bones.*

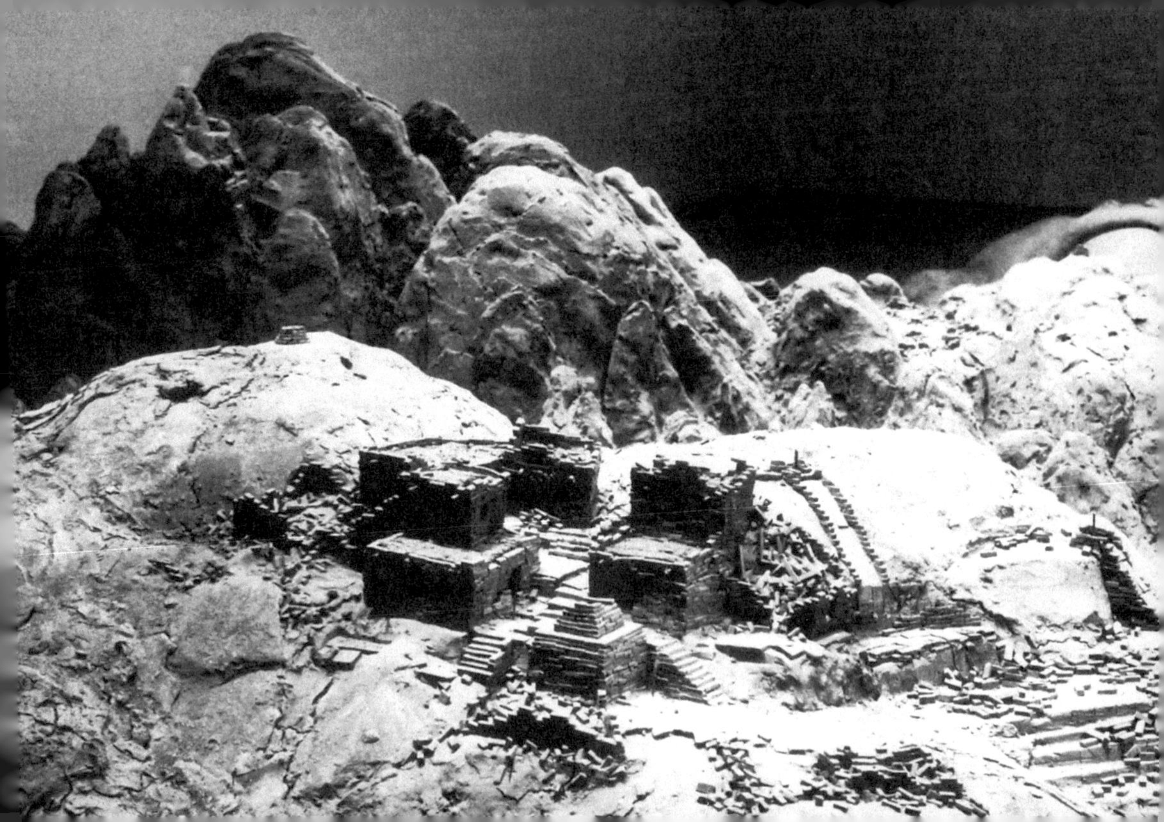

For almost a mile, nothing but leg bones—the patella, then the femur, and then further to the west, pelvic bones—mixed male and female—then ribs, and vertebrae, and so on, until it became obvious that we were unearthing a great skeleton drawn on the earth. Like a gigantic fossil, the collective imprint of a communal body. Did the souls of the dead merge as well? Reborn when reincorporated into the anatomy? Was the skeleton fleshed with earth? What then is the role of the incinerator with its bowls of grain, its viscera, its cremations, its excrement at the center? And the field of regular round hills, half out of the earth like growing tubers, surrounded by sharp spears. Is this a garden or a graveyard?

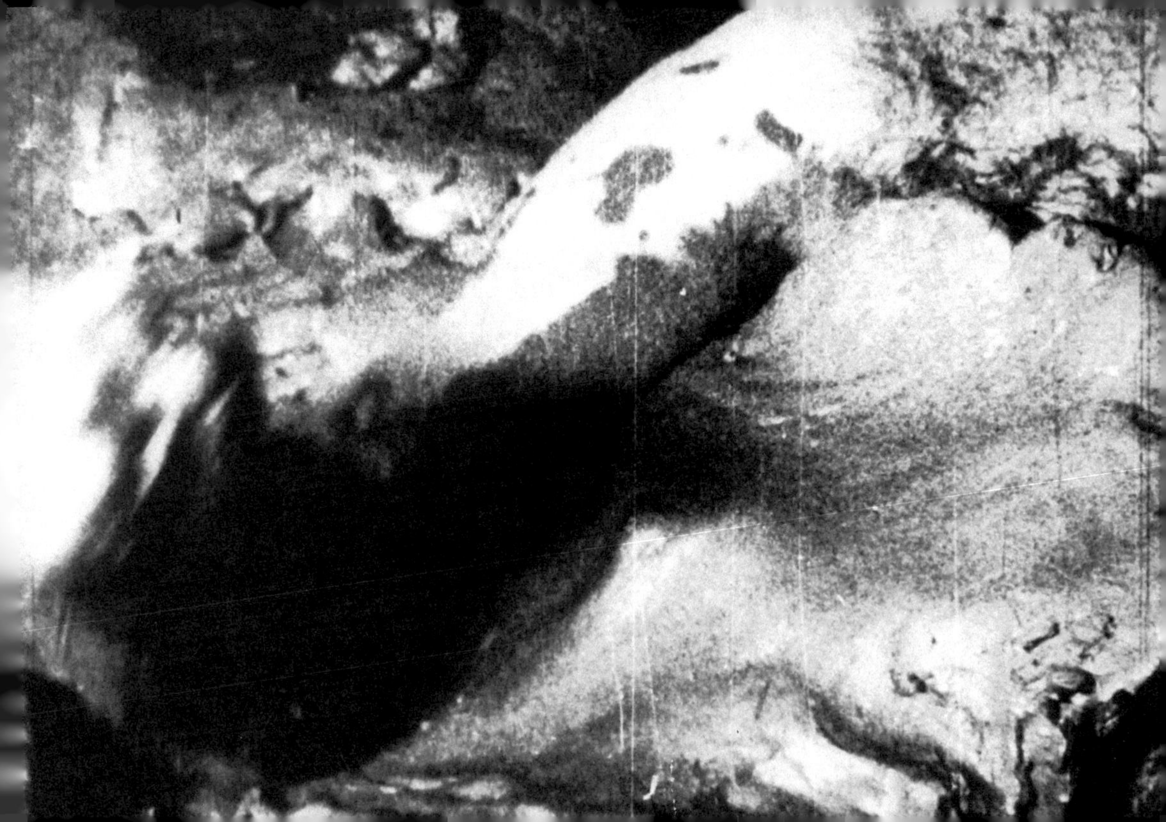

August 4: I dreamed I was a little girl and an old woman talked to me, her hand on my shoulder, on my knee. I was a little boy and she a man and as the dream went on I couldn't tell the women from the men or the men from the women. Telling time. S/he was telling me time. I awoke with this phrase ringing in my ears, divorced from its ordinary meaning. S/he told me time on a great shadowed dial that lay on the land, moving sunwise. The story drifts beyond my words. Something about digging deeper, a breathing body covered in earth, trees making love to the underground streams from which they sprang, the rise of hills like bubbles beneath cities and children's laughter, about stars leaving shadows on the plains, an armored belly digesting past and future. And about the people who made the paths, the travellers whose wanderings, if ceased, would end the world.

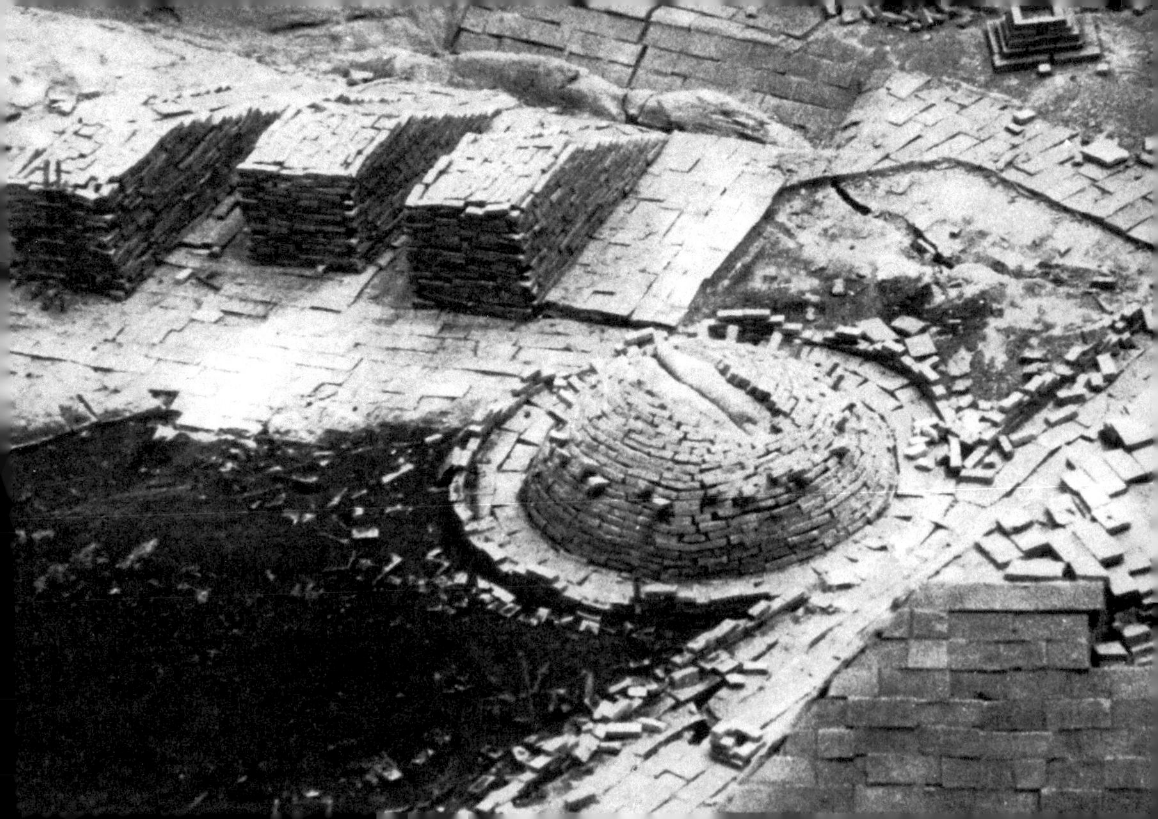

August 12: We return to the road dwelling, ostensibly to look for snakes. A holiday. But this is not a road at all. Its curve is now a straight fast line. It has become dots and dashes, with intervals that barely exist. From these towers something flew across the spaces. Banners? Birds? Beacons? Yes. The towers are filled with charcoal. Beacons beaming from past to present and back again. The people came this way on the dwelling road, settled, some sooner, some later. The fires beckoned others, burned to make the route from circle to triangle to square and back to circle. With the dead as guides. As burning signals to the living. Not sacrifices, but willing scouts to ashfilled wells. From the towers as from the mountain top they could see the great skeleton. Or had they turned their backs by then?

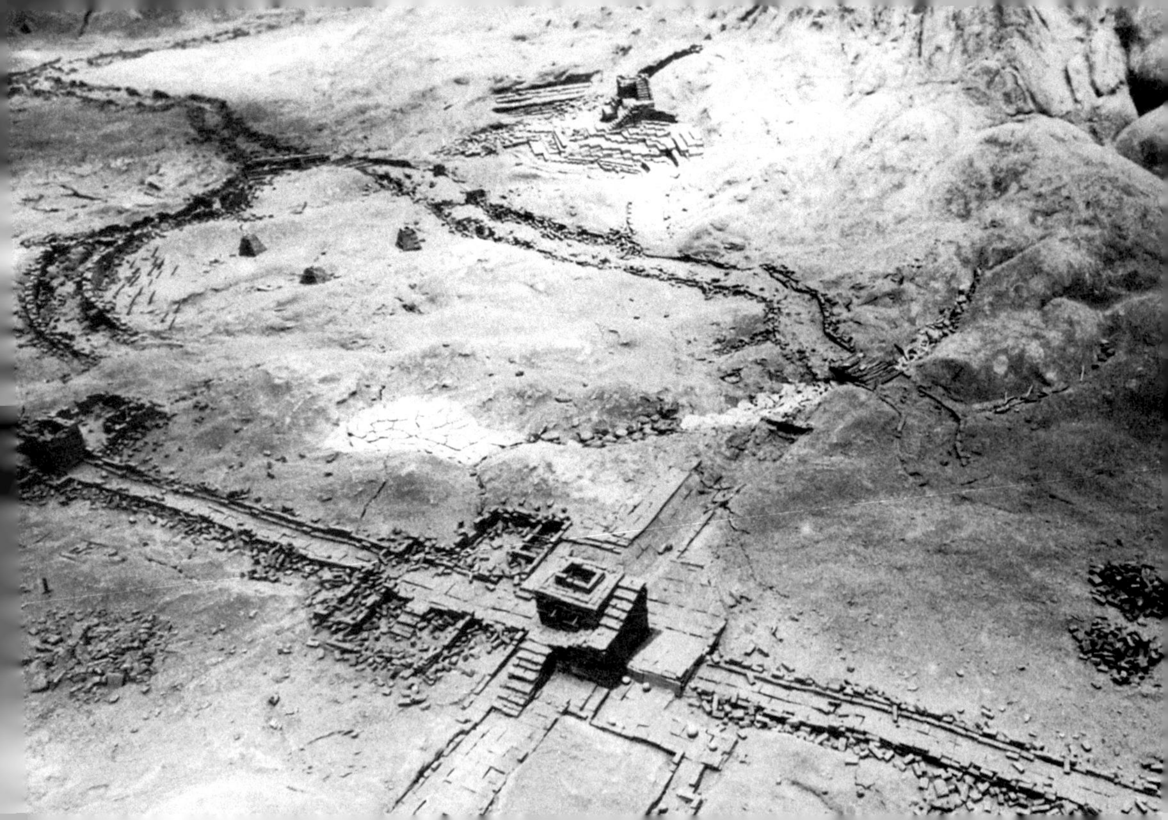

August 29: Strange that such sameness can change so quickly, such monotony can vary so extremely. Yet as the seasons change we're in new places, the terrain seems to respond to some new viewpoint. The beginnings of the road dwelling near the wrinkled old hills containing the triangular caves runs downhill to the beginnings of the rooms, uphill, then down again to where the road turns straight or back along the other routes to the ziggurat incinerators at the foot of the mountain. Across the great skeleton to the stone-domed ritual mounds, the stake forest, the prurient tumescences, on to the circular city, and on around the mountain to the growing bricks, still growing in their decay, to the spiral ruin—decay epitomized—to the later city on the hill, the dullest place, the farthest corner of the map, past the paved and ramped mysteriously functional buildings and back around the mountain to the caves again. It all sounds downright simple, clear, well-mapped and reasonable. But one day a vista will open where there was none before, a hill rise where it was flat. As colors change the land itself transforms. We circle the mountain a different way each journey.

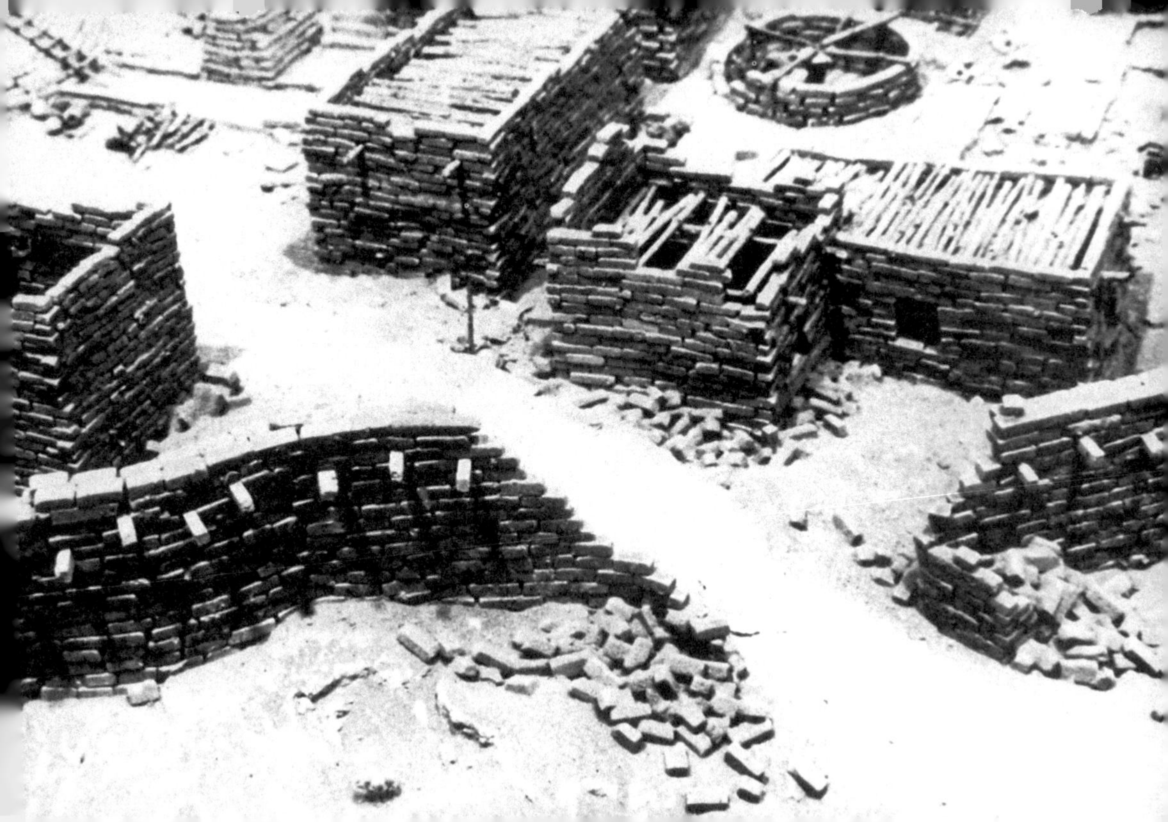

A hundred miles one day, ten the next. Uphill down and downhill up, today. Tomorrow winter.

X clutches his map and makes witty, worried comments about how different everything looks in different lights. The needle on our compass swings to point us where it leads—today to the spiral, which we had not intended to explore until the circular excavations were completed. Tomorrow back to the shards beneath the incinerator, which we thought we had exhausted. There I found your latest message.

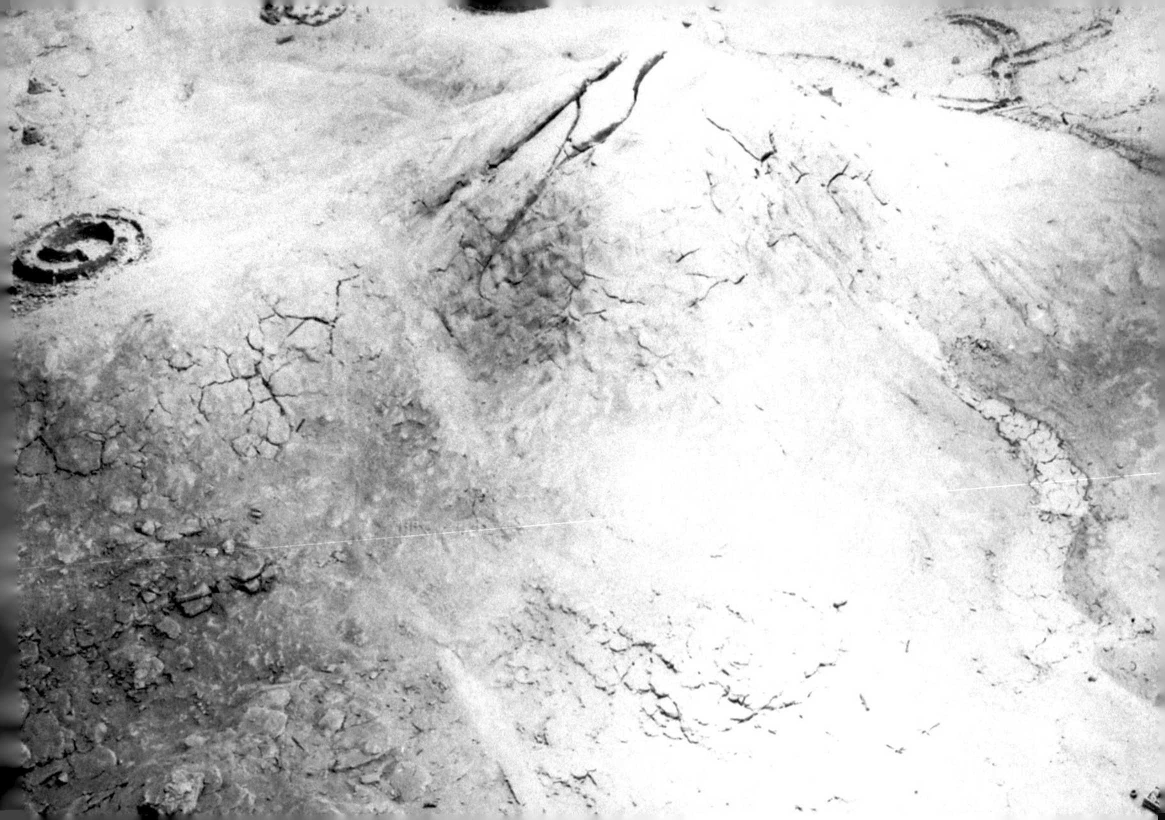

Ideas? What do you call ideas? Something of no substance? We have nothing of no substance. Everything we know we hear, see, sense, taste, touch. The sun moves, the moon and the stars. The waters and the energy beneath the earth are encouraged to rise as circle, spiral, line. The births and deaths of the people and the land. Then the births again. Surely these are not what you call ideas? They are things of substance. They are real.

September 8: It's all happening at once. This place is tugged back and forth between extremes as though by sealess tides. The very richness of our finds frustrates linear interpretation. Every theory is shattered by the next discovery. Every clue contradicts the last.
When did the break come?
When did the camouflage fall away and the towers begin to rise as high as the hills? When did the temples separate themselves from the dwellings, from their sites?

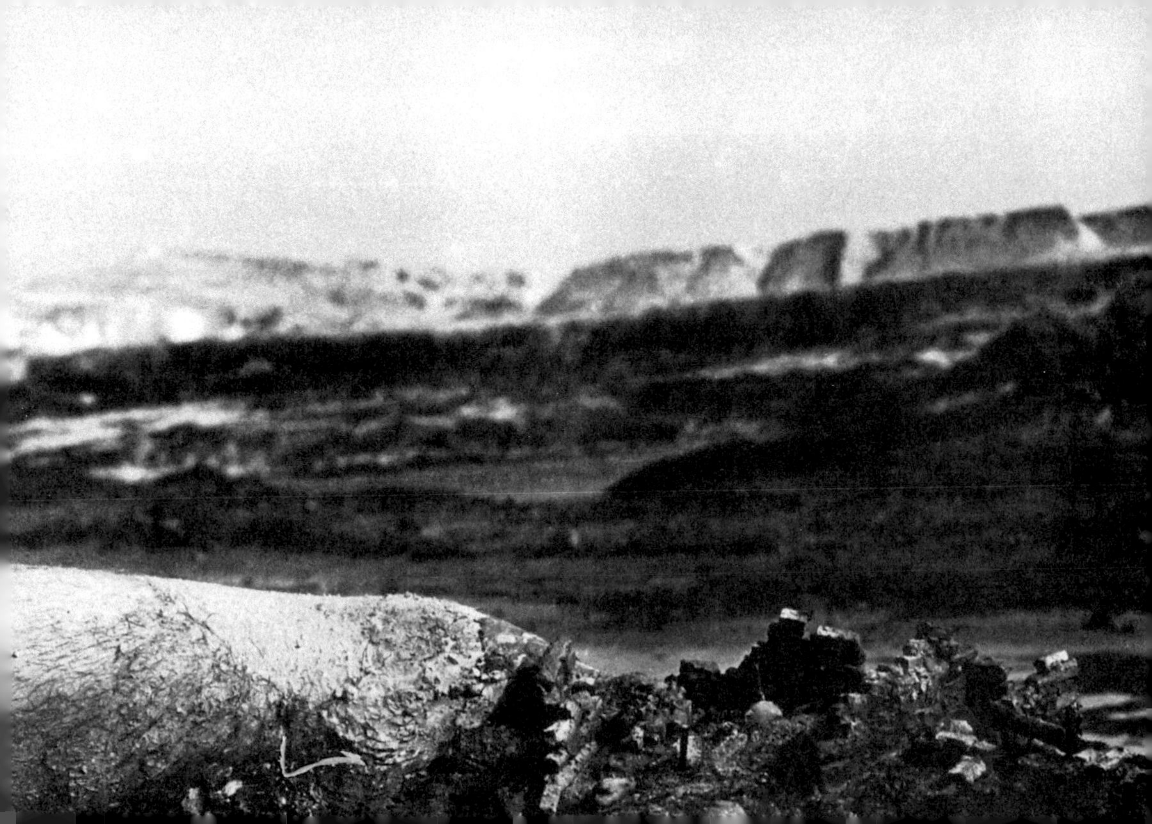

When did the people dangerously assert their independence?

No chronology emerges, or rather what emerges is an impossible superimposition, simultaneous history. It's all very confusing. And for some reason the confusion does not disturb me. X says we are here to find answers, not more questions. My happiness irritates him. He is suffering from betrayal. Logic is laughing at him.

September 20: I dreamed of a clock without numbers. I dreamed of numbers that grew and changed. I dreamed of a line with no end, and I am still dreaming of the journey.

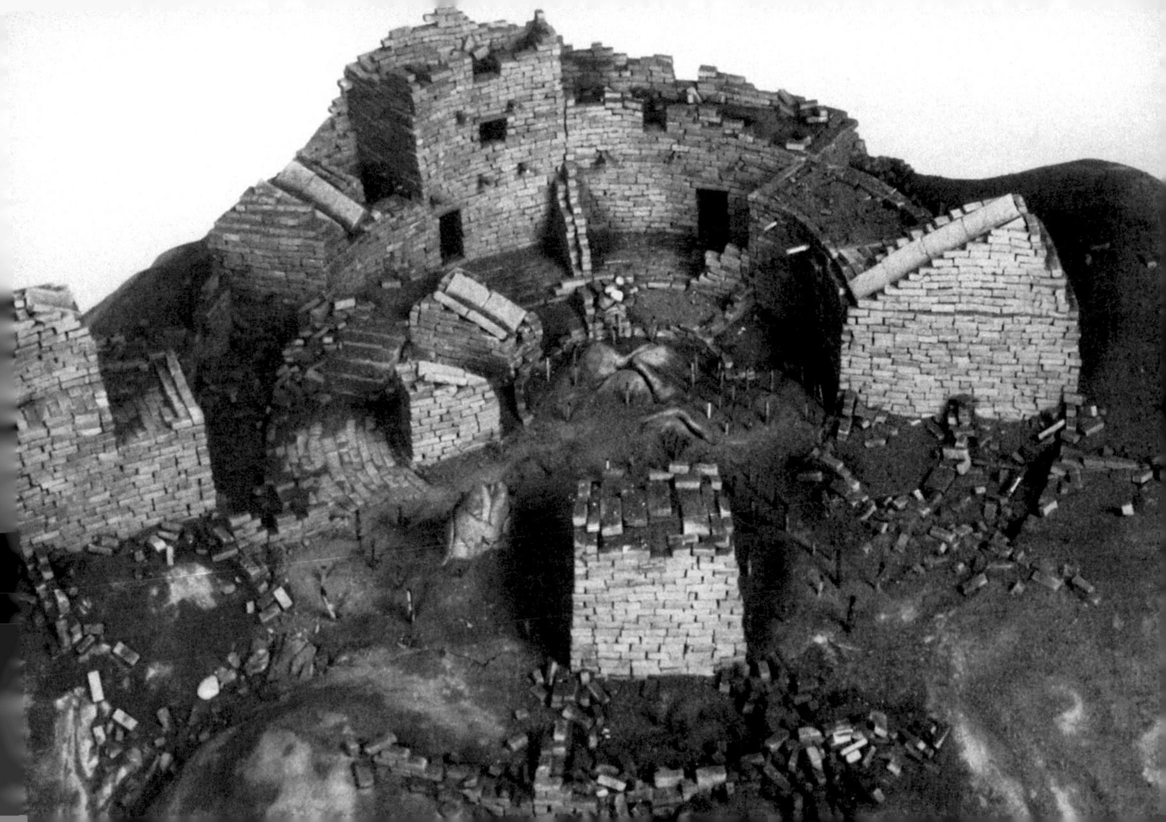

In the old days we penetrated the mountain. Now the secret is lost. We pay homage to its memory by building our own hills, fearing the oldest, deepest passage. Domed like the mother's body, they suffice to bring the sun each day, and the seasons of arid waiting, growth, decay. But the extraordinary can be met only by the extraordinary. When the night swallows the day in midlife, when the earth's shadow crosses the sun as well as the moon, when the light fades, we will have to rediscover the entrance. The secret was drawn in lines on the earth and in the sky and no one reads them any more. Because the waters dried up. When they were parted by dreams we could see the other life again. The black bogs have stolen our waters as the skies stole our milk. The best place to study the stars is from a hole in the earth.

Do you hear us? Do you see me?

This is the time of year when we join hands and dance all night around the hills we've made. When our population grows or dwindles a new hill is built to our size. It is very important that no link between the numbers be loosened. An unused hill may be re-integrated in coming years. If not, its number is lost. One

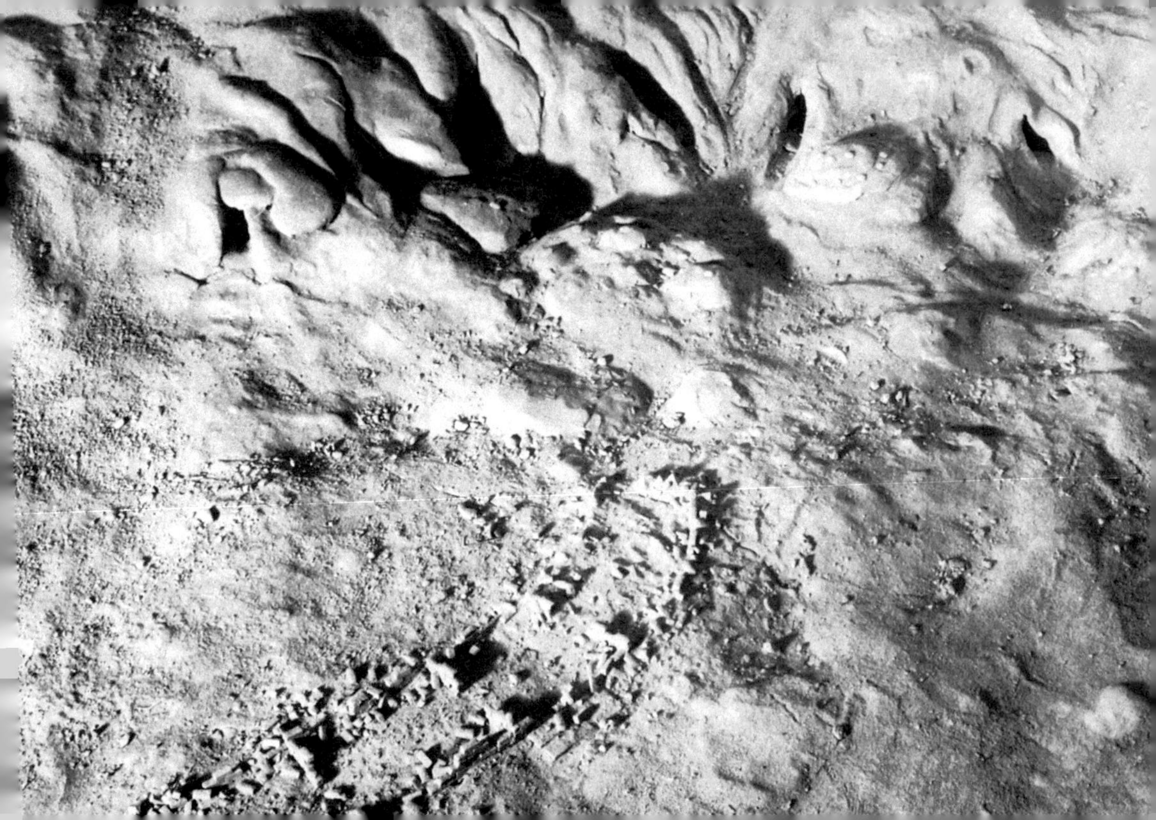

pair of childbearing age is chosen to confirm the transitory nature of the present number, climbing into the cleft of the hill's summit, acknowledging the change that may result.
Speak up. Come closer. Are you my past or my future?

Sept. 16: X says I am getting worse. I'm "too involved". I reply that there is no such thing as being too involved in one's chosen work. He says passion is useless in archeology. I say archeology, like everything else, is useless without passion. He says that is a typically female sentiment. I say the people—all the people, men and women—would have understood such passion far better than his way which omits more than it accepts.
I keep to myself my suspicion that the inhabitants of what we see as ruins have perfected an androgyny with no resemblance to the unreconciled dualities we hide behind that term. I do not tell him I am dreaming. I do not tell him that I dream each woman and each man is man and woman depending on the time of day or year or the activity s/he is engaged in at the time.

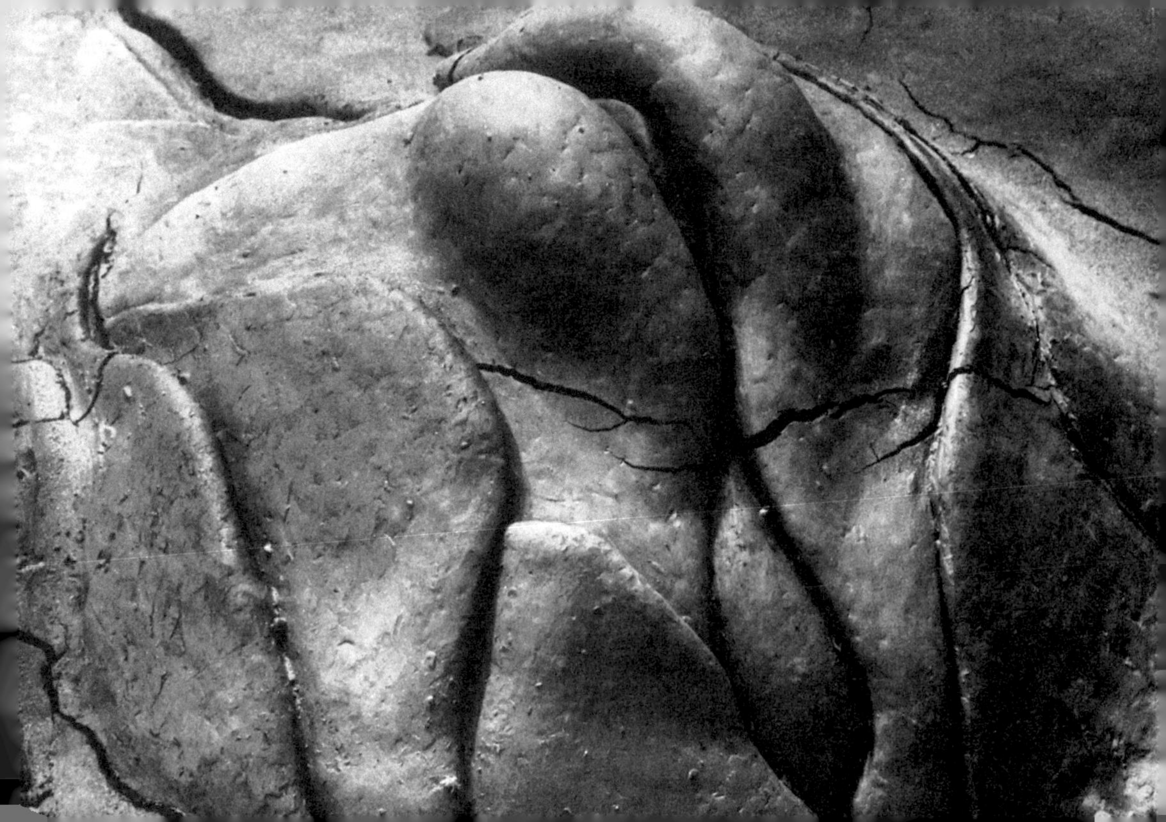

That these dreams, or messages, are confirmed by the ways in which the landscape where we work has been transformed. That I dream and then we excavate my memories. That my dreams are preceded by a different sort of vision—highly detailed stills accompanied sometimes by an isolated phrase—visions rising just before I sleep or wake, in that twilight time between times. I do not tell him these beads are strung into a tale where everything happens at once. I do not tell him that I have stopped thinking in terms of myths, because they are reality.

It must be autumn. The first berries leave purple blood on our hands.

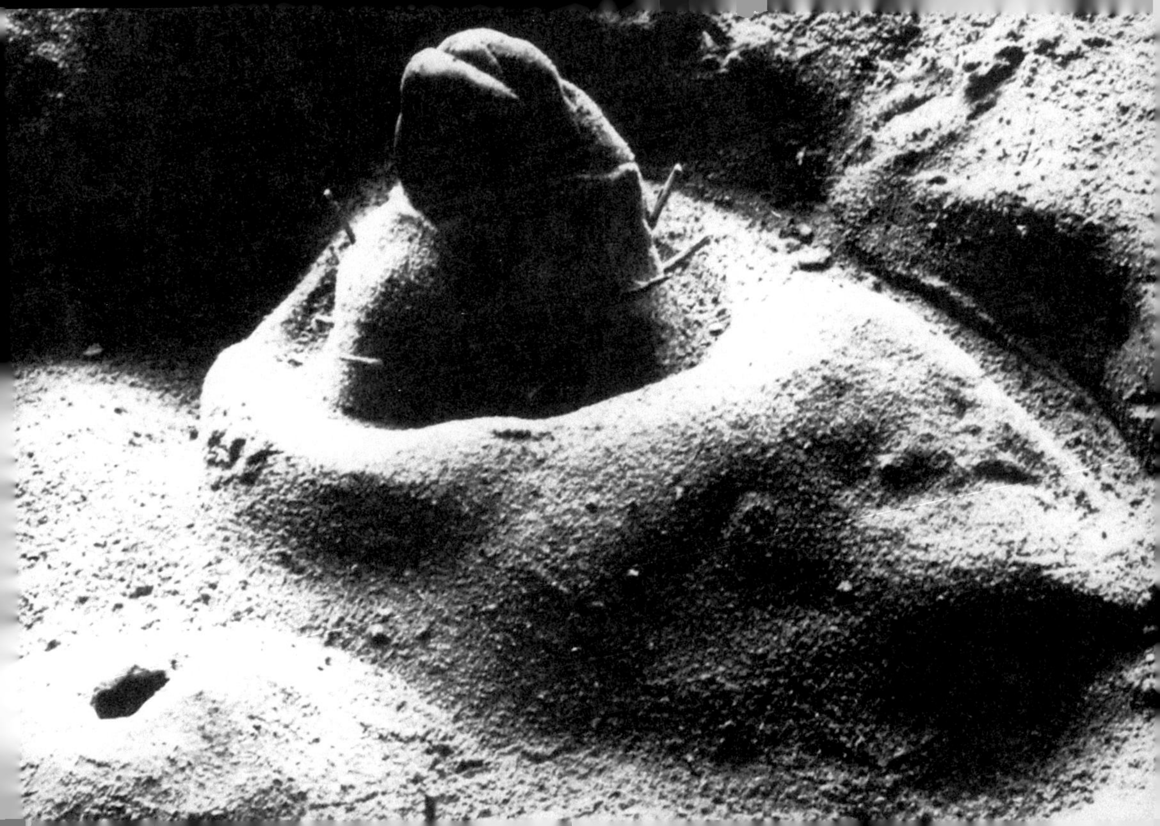

September 27: Last night I dreamed a warning. Sometimes I lie in bed, hovering between wakefulness and sleep, and one of my limbs—a distant one, a leg or hand—will suddenly begin to grow. It is an uneasy but not unpleasant sensation, like walking closer to one's own body, which nears as it expands, inflating gently, but also gaining mass, getting heavier and heavier ... Since we came here this experience has taken on a new dimension. The distant limb becomes so large it is a landscape and I can feel the hairs stand up like trees. Last night I fell asleep and this process continued. I was a house. I grew to such immense dimensions that the people entered and inhabited me. I have no clear image as to what sort of house I was. Maybe I was shaped as I am, like the temples in forms of god or goddess where people go to sleep and dream.

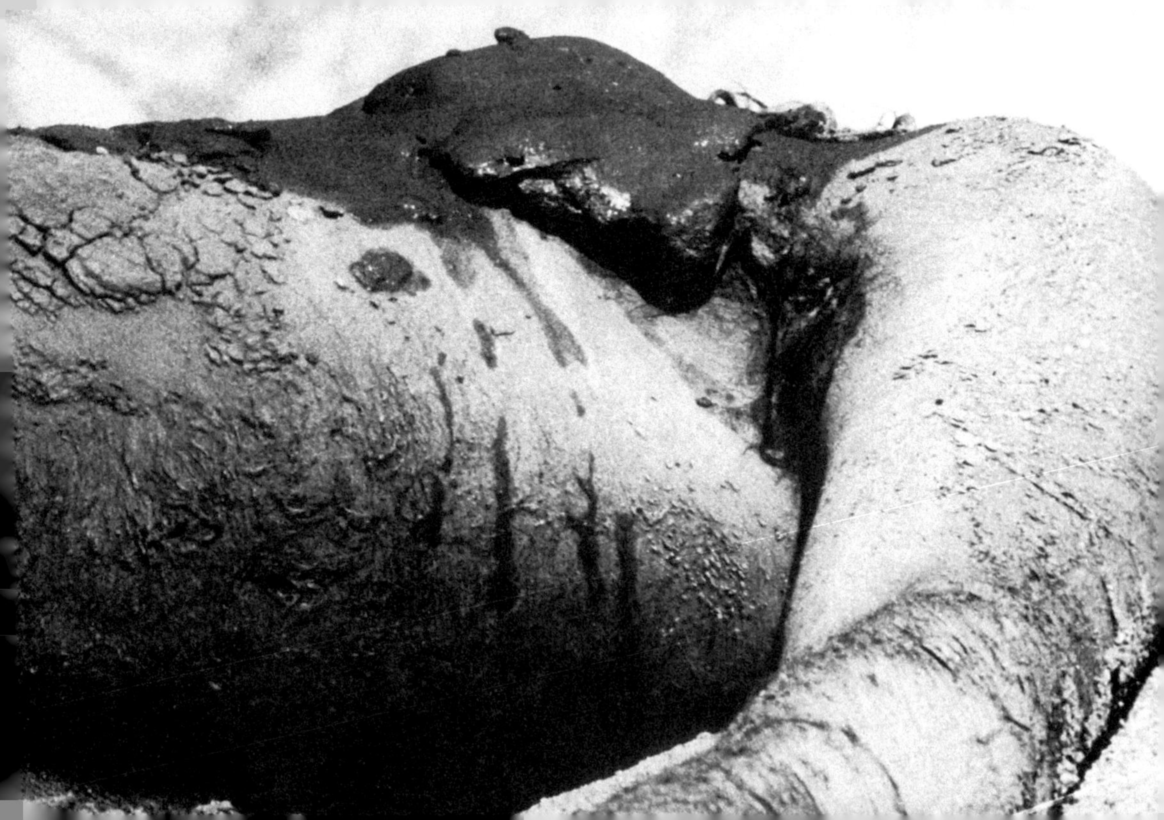

Maybe I was curved around myself, knees drawn up to my chin and my belly the center. They came in huge crowds, streaming down from the hills to enter me, and I was ecstatic. I was *filled* in some way that transcended sex and pregnancy. Eventually I filled so full that I exploded, shattered into a thousand pieces which I saw disappearing like points of light into darkness around me. The fragments were both the people and myself, both flesh and turf, fruit and seed.

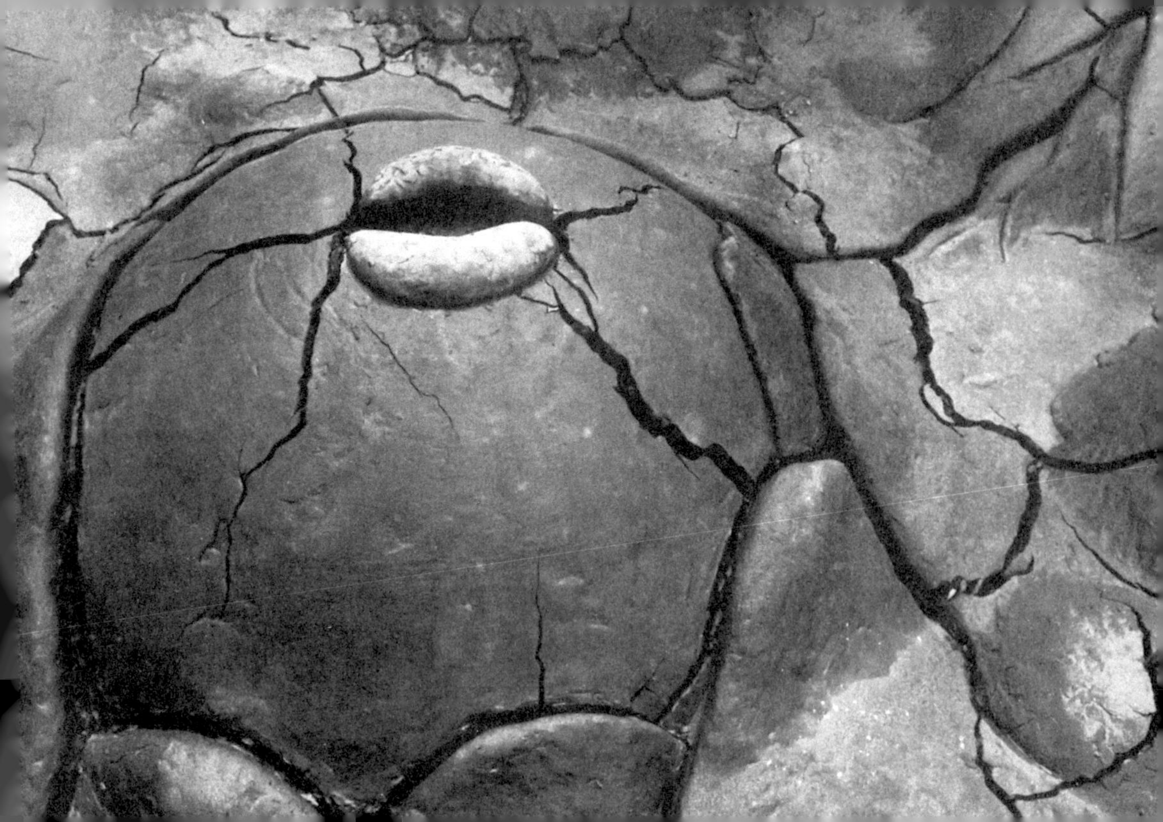

When did we find those rounded bricks of earth containing seeds? X was trying to specify the agricultural technique. They lay at a respectful distance from every other remain. They were sparse and roughly in a circle, but surely too far apart, too few, to have been building units? One of the seeds had blossomed, berried. When did we find them? Or were they always with us?
Lost. Every hill the same. Each one my mirror. The distances the same and not the same. I walk. I circle. I do not go toward the cavern in the mountain but now and then it is in front of me. I change direction. Lost again. A soothing motion. From here to there. Why is my lack of progress not more frustrating? Why have I shed all the anxiety of the last few weeks? I think I hear a bell ringing, a bell of clay. Earth against earth. The sun is behind the clouds blurring my landmarks. I think I hear water running. Footsteps. Home is that way, but where is home?

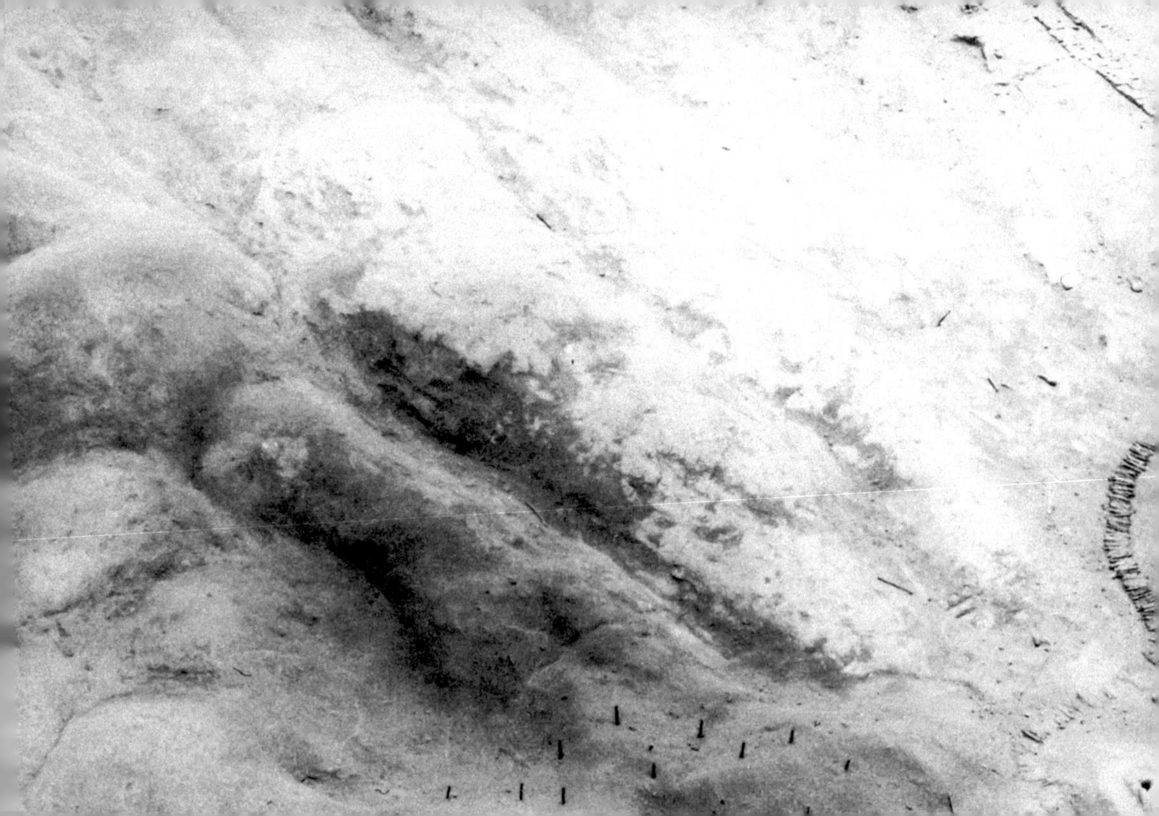

The day the fires began. Listen closely. The first one fell from the sky. No, the first blew up from the seething core. The first sparked when two bodies rubbed together. The first was kindled from the bones of a murderer. The first was glowing underwater in the eye of the horse, the ox, the serpent, the deer, the dolphin. There was no second. No one was without a fire to nurture. The land lit up with signals from people to people, family to family, person to person, echoing networks in the sky and mysterious beams from the swamps. From hill to tower to wall to cliff. The rituals followed later, when the first fire was forgotten.

October 4: It's all happening at once. I am haunted, as is X, who won't admit it, by the great petaled towers giving birth to something sexual but genderless. How could we have missed them in our early surveys? The geologists are baffled and have called in the biologists because it seems these monstrous growths were once plants, now obscenely pink and petrified. The engineers consult dolefully with the geologists over other formations.

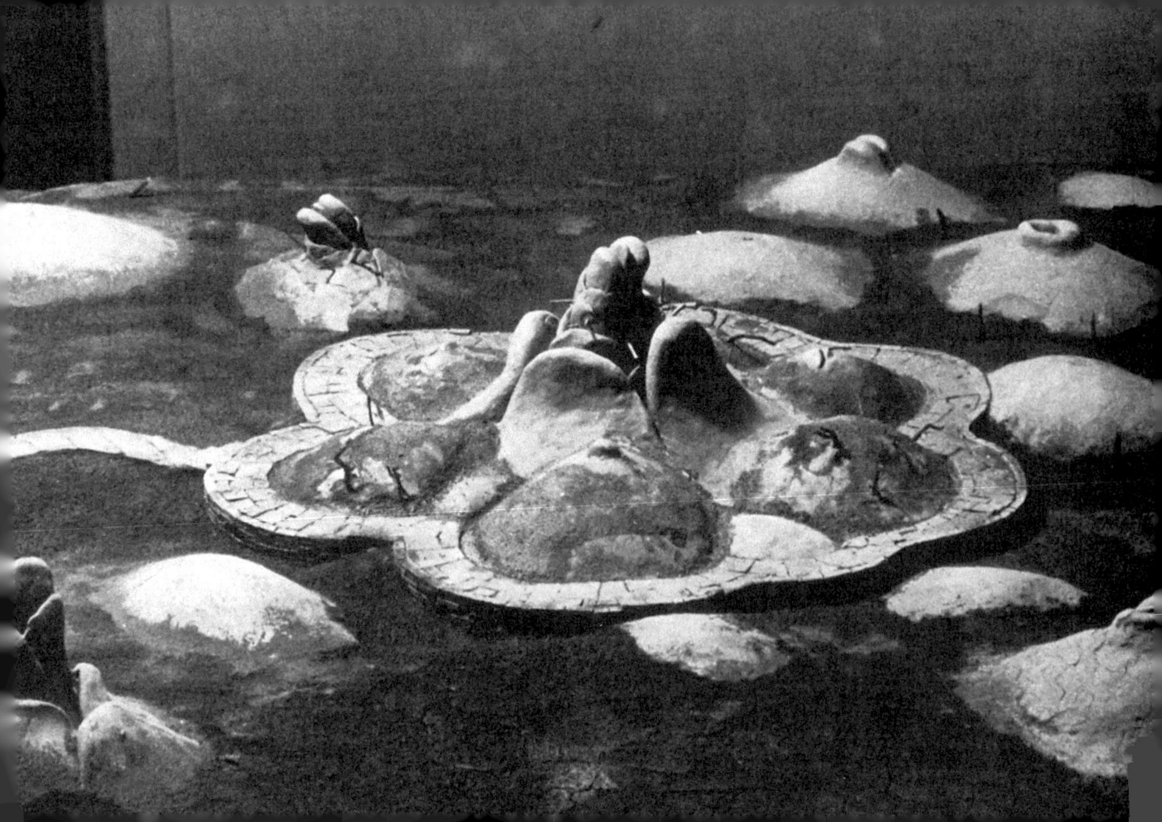

Since they reject the possibility of a "primitive" people mastering such massive construction, they must explain them as natural phenomena—no mean task. The iconographers huddle over the undulating lines on the exteriors of the vessels containing the messages. Perhaps they echo the waves of a long-gone sea; then again, they might represent the tremors of the restless earth; or mean nothing— pleasing decoration. Rain is remembered only in the stalactites dripping from the roof of the cave; or are those rapid lines across the bricks ... The astronomers, at least, to X's discomfort, are confirming the lunar and stellar alignments from the observatory, the highly sophisticated use of declinations, azimuths, and other facts so precise their vagueness is not yet recognized. No one can explain the incoherent readings of telluric magnetism near the seeded bricks.

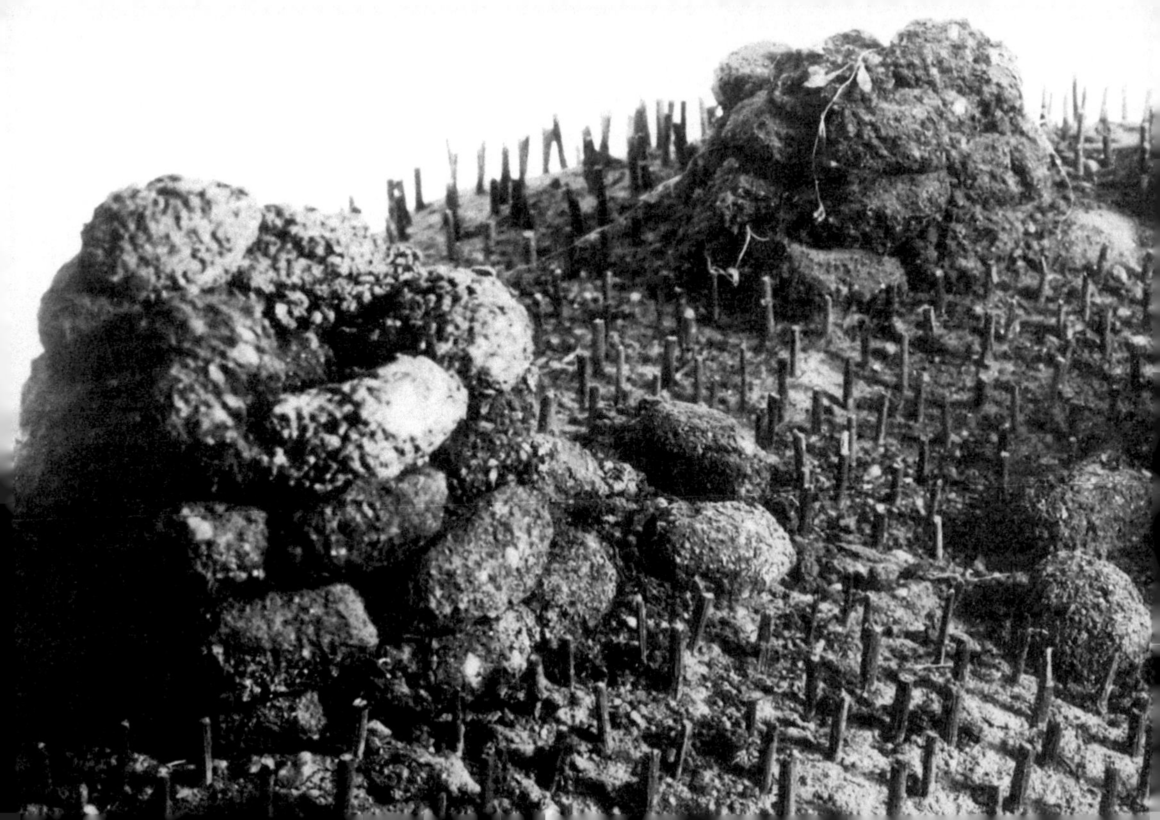

Oh yes. Things are getting out of hand. Who made that gaping leering mouth or sex? The women? Sheila na gig and Magog? Sisters in the silly season? Or the men watching the earth open and close and tremble with temptation? Who made that flaccid tower, so far from the rooted mound? Was it created at a moment of arousal or satiation? Its crevice imitating, desiring, or becoming the other?

So it was you.

Your touch I felt in my dreams. Your words reaching me through marks in the dust. Your body, your bodies, I caressed with my digging fingertips, brushing gently with tiny sharpnesses your bones and bricks. You add yourself to yourselves and to myselves. You stretch further and pile higher. You gobble the past greedily and excrete the future. Playing with these parts of yourselves.

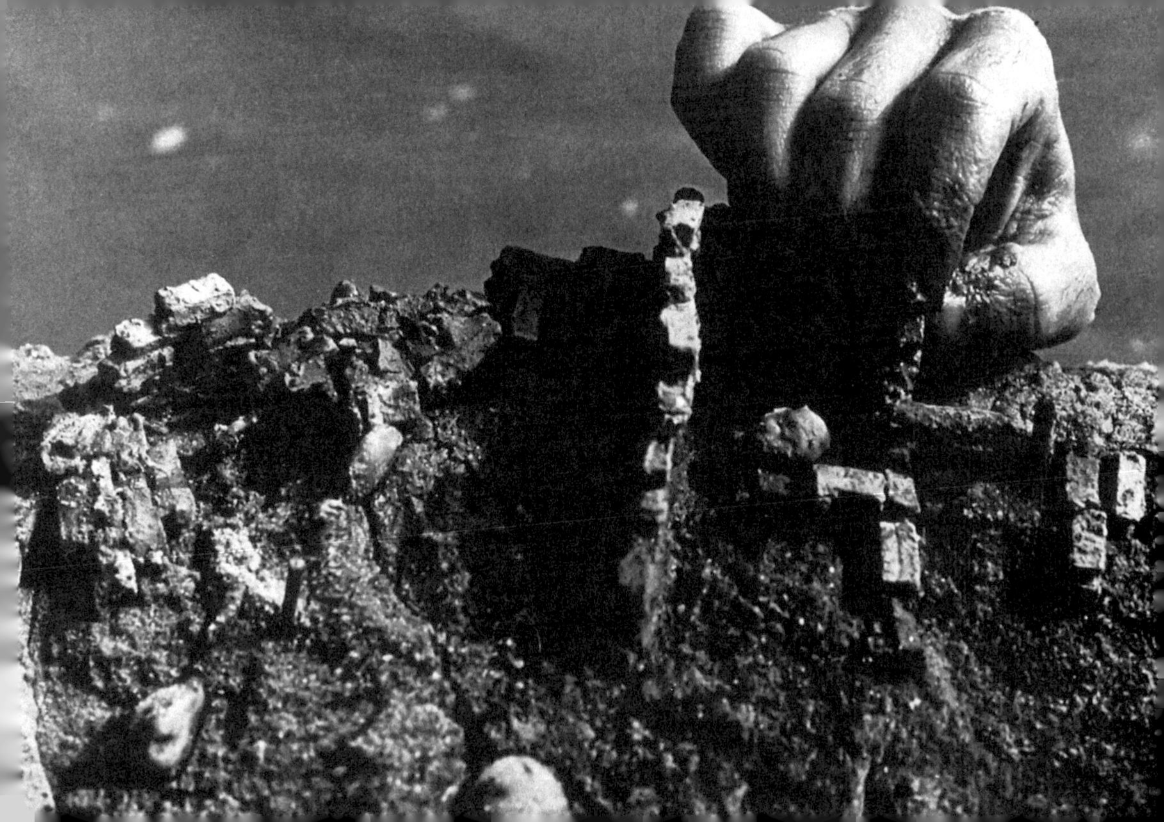

Ladder, darkness, round pebbles cool to the touch. Seeds in winter. Here in this place I am larger than life, but over there an ant hill looms over me. The pulse is contained here. The stream is warm and sticky. The walls grow and crumble and we share the feast. There are two of us. The soft part of my foot is the rung of the ladder. A tree reaches from here to there, flowering at the top where the light is, woven below into a mass of tendrils weaving with other veins the web that forms the world below the one we live on.

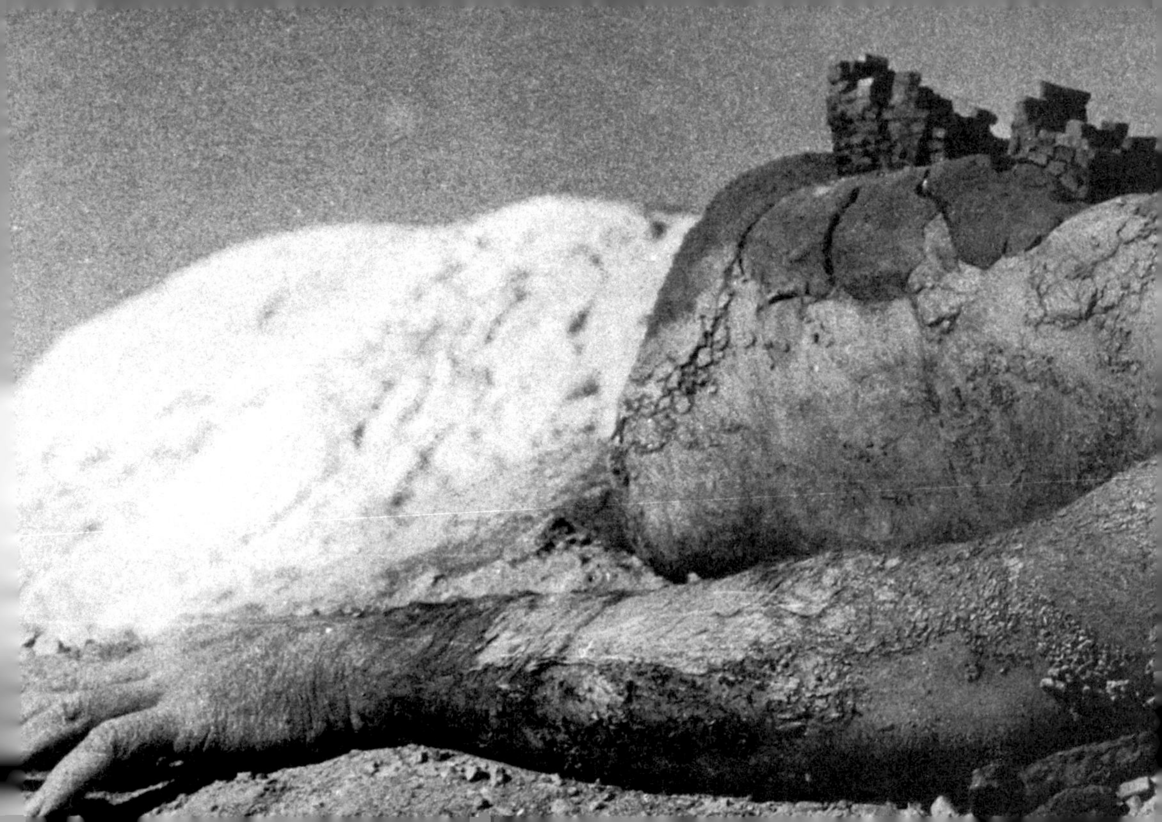

The son thrashing on the body of his mother re-envelops himself in earth. Seeks the waters. But now they are gone. The sea is sucked back. Parched life. The people are gone. When we mourn we cover ourselves with mud and when it has cracked and fallen away we resume our lives without you.
He rises and casts off the earth that clings to him. He rises in a new skin.
He towers above the land. He begins to build. To build hills and then towers. To send signals. He forgets the holes. He builds straight lines from curves. But in time the straight lines too begin to wander, meander, return to their beginnings. Are you listening? Can you hear?
Yes. At last I can hear.

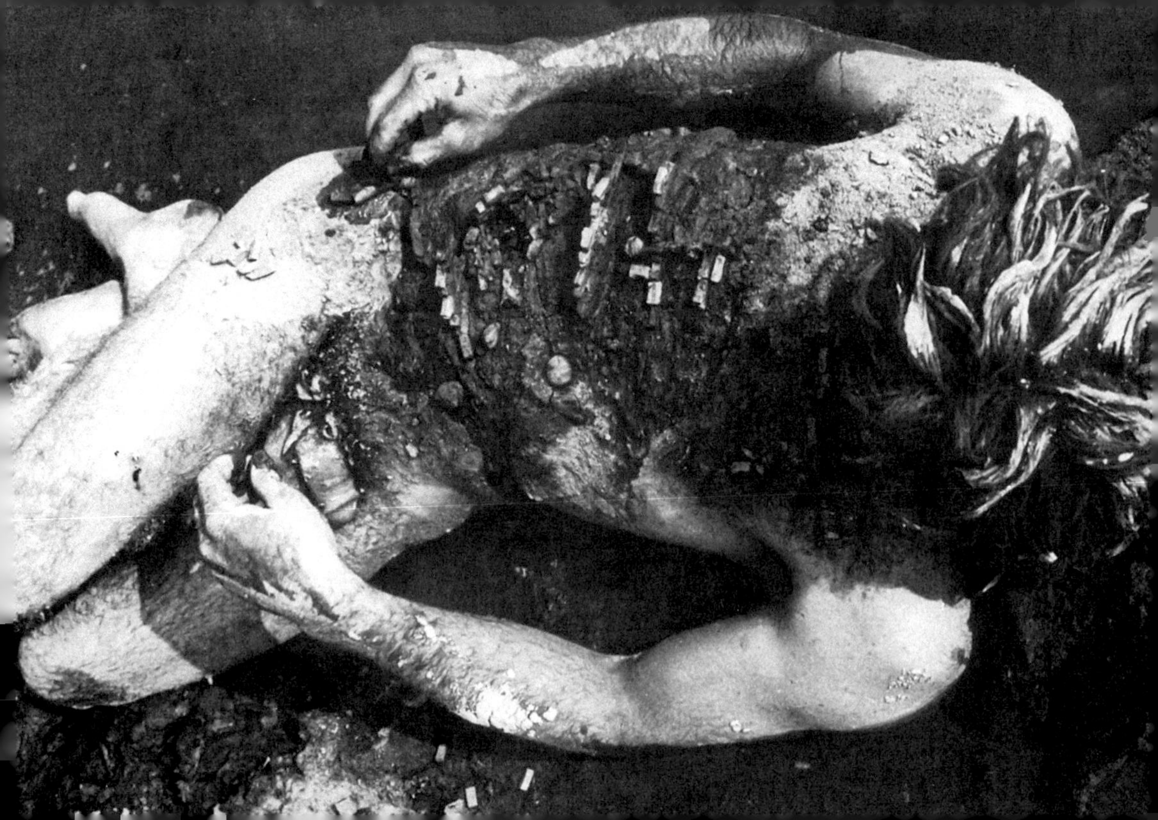

October 15: X was fortunately not in camp when they were delivered. They are hidden in my tent. I can hear them moving dryly from one side of the cages to the other, dryly but smoothly, pacing the measure of their prison. Like the seeds hidden in bricks. In time. Those with claws and heavier tails make an older, more erratic sound. But it is the legless ones that haunt me. I see them coiled and waiting, armored in luminous scales, imitating the springs below them. You told me to bring them back to complete the circle and revive the powers but I'm afraid they'll turn on me. Absurd. I dream of fields of them moving gracefully beneath my buttocks. It is not quite a nightmare. You are there.

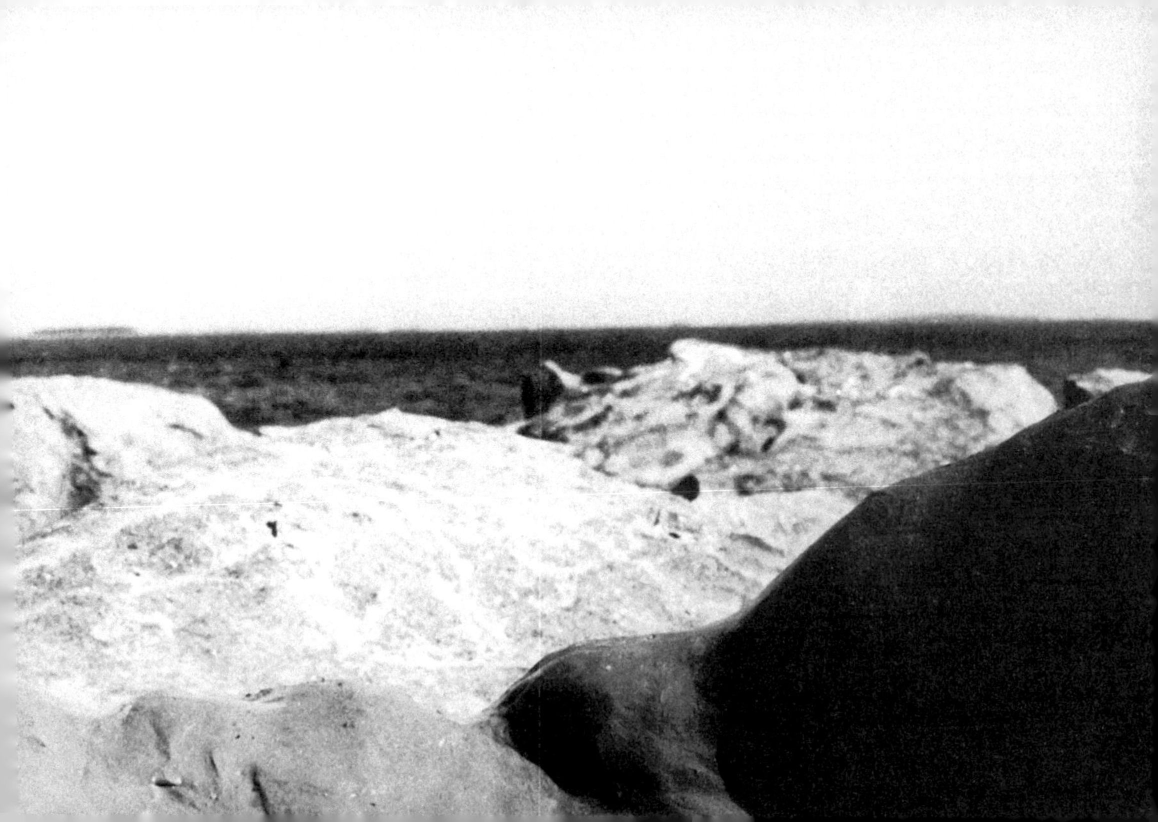

Today I saw your footprints in the dust, your handprint on the wall, but I breathed out quickly and erased you before X saw them. It is better that you come only at night, that your parched red body enters mine only in the sweet damp blackness where the snakes rustle below us. Why do you ask me to dig deeper in some places, and leave others alone?

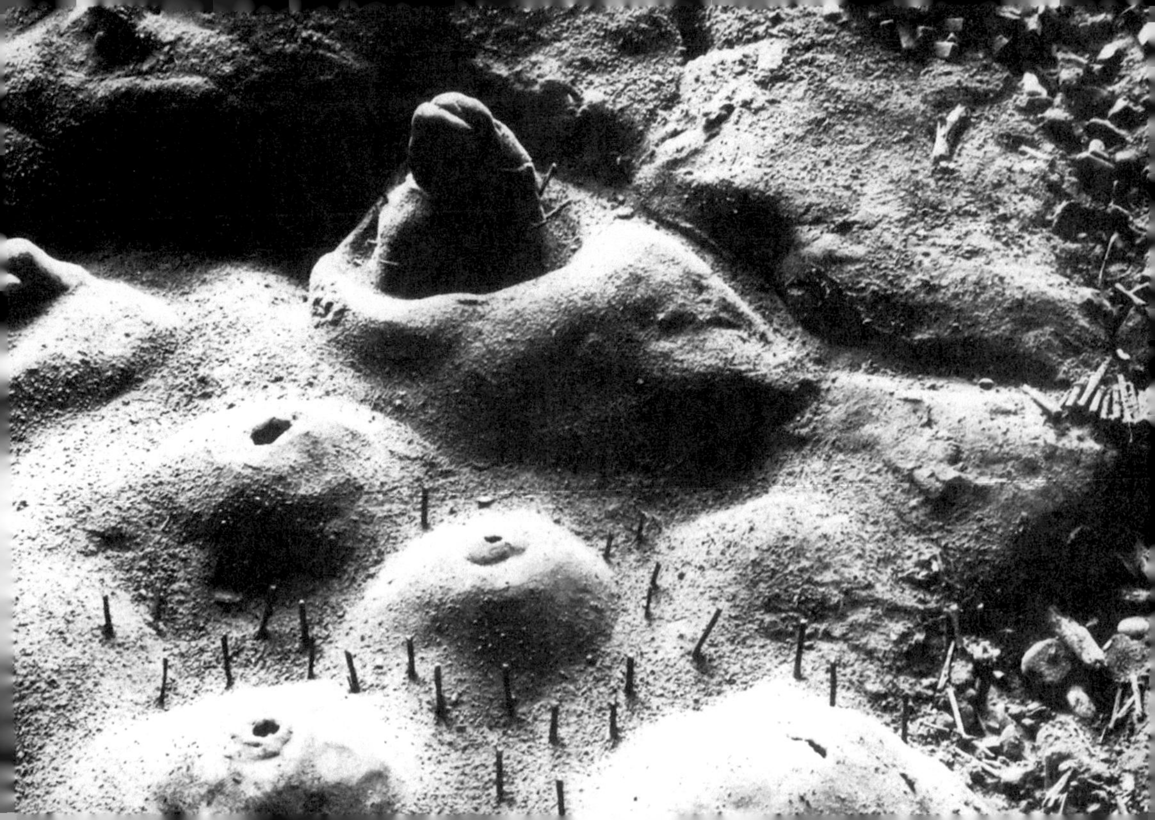

These rituals have all been dreamt by someone somewhere, passing from repetition to reality through my quivering brain. The new is only as new as the sun rising each morning and the moon pulling the tides freshly over the sands.

The old is only as old as the time it takes for dark to become light. With our shovels and compasses, our measures and our picks, we touch your bones, without sensing the life left in them. Which of its many forms will your knowledge take for us?

It will have to be as long and sharp and narrow as a needle if you are to feel it.

No, it is a sea of needles, pricking every pore at once. Through my lacy flesh a cleansing stream will flow. Are you still waiting for me?

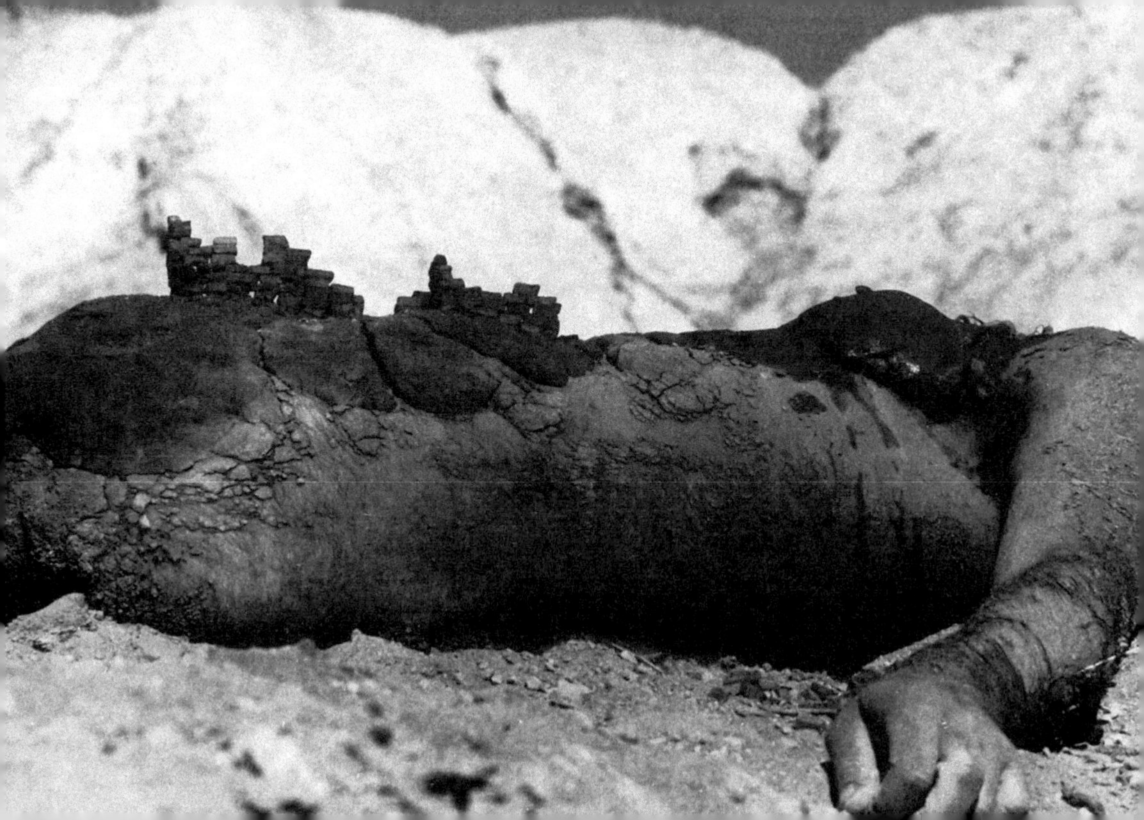

October 17: X pounces on it, quickly, fearfully, before he can wonder. Little numbers track across all surfaces, grids with axes crossing ours. He will freeze this hot red place into black and white and gray and black on white. In the name of the logical gods he will isolate the particles in glass cases, in computers, splay and expose them under lenses too powerful to perceive their variety, remove their power to fertilize each other. He wants to take it all away in pictures. I want to leave the life in this place. It may be the last place to live.

October 19: Today I brought my diaries to the field instead of my notes. X asked sarcastically if I were writing poetry.

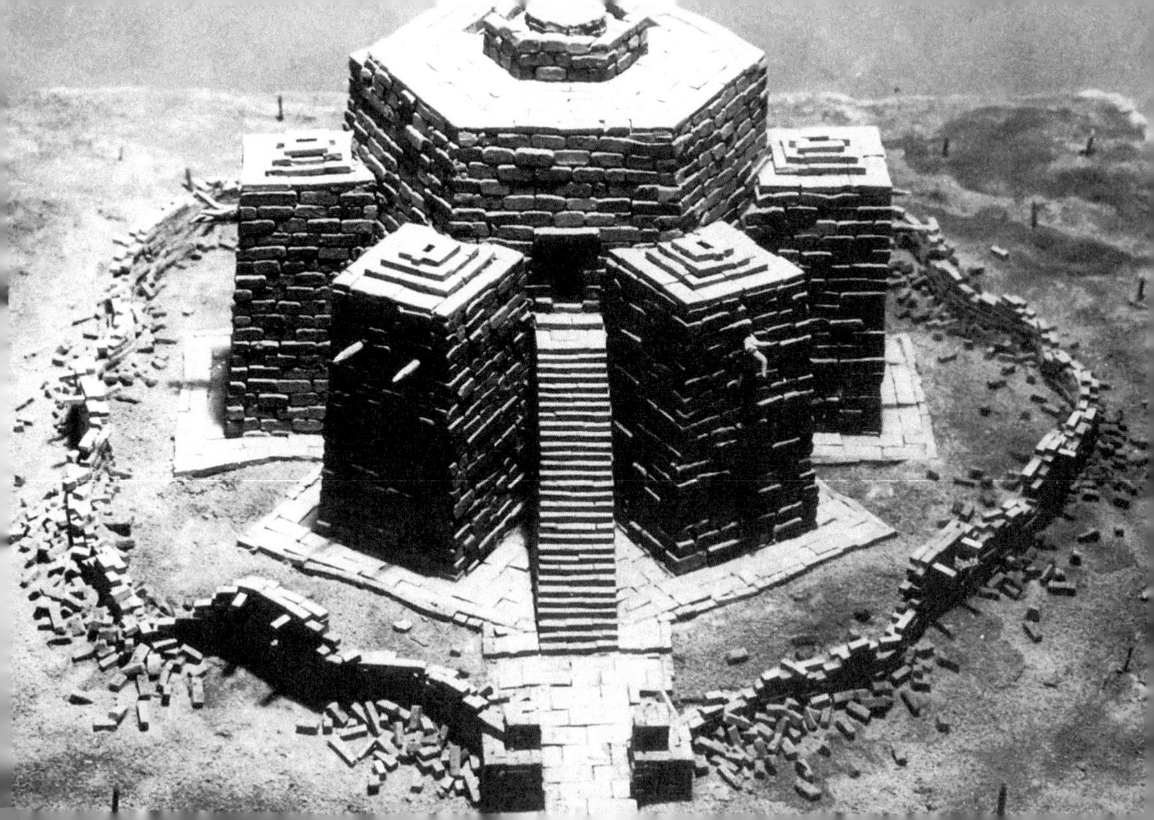

I keep watch outside here, with my dreams and illusions, my feet in the mud of today. Is inside ahead or behind or beyond me? You beckon, but I will be useless to your fires if I can't stay outside. With a view inside. One eye a telescope the other a microscope. I look through an unglassed window that seems both very close and very far away. Inside it is cool and dim and very quiet, streaks of sunlight stretching across a hard dirt floor. In the far corner lies a bowl, a perfect semisphere, balanced delicately on one point. I can just discern the characters that cover its inside surface, but of course I cannot read them.

When the snakes uncoil the mother cries no more.

October 20: Turn the pages faster, faster. Flip the ages over to catch the right that hides beneath the verse.

You wear masks, don't you? Skins which you shed each year like a snake's.

Off with your head. On with a new one. Harvest holds true.

I-dollies buried in the ritual gardens.

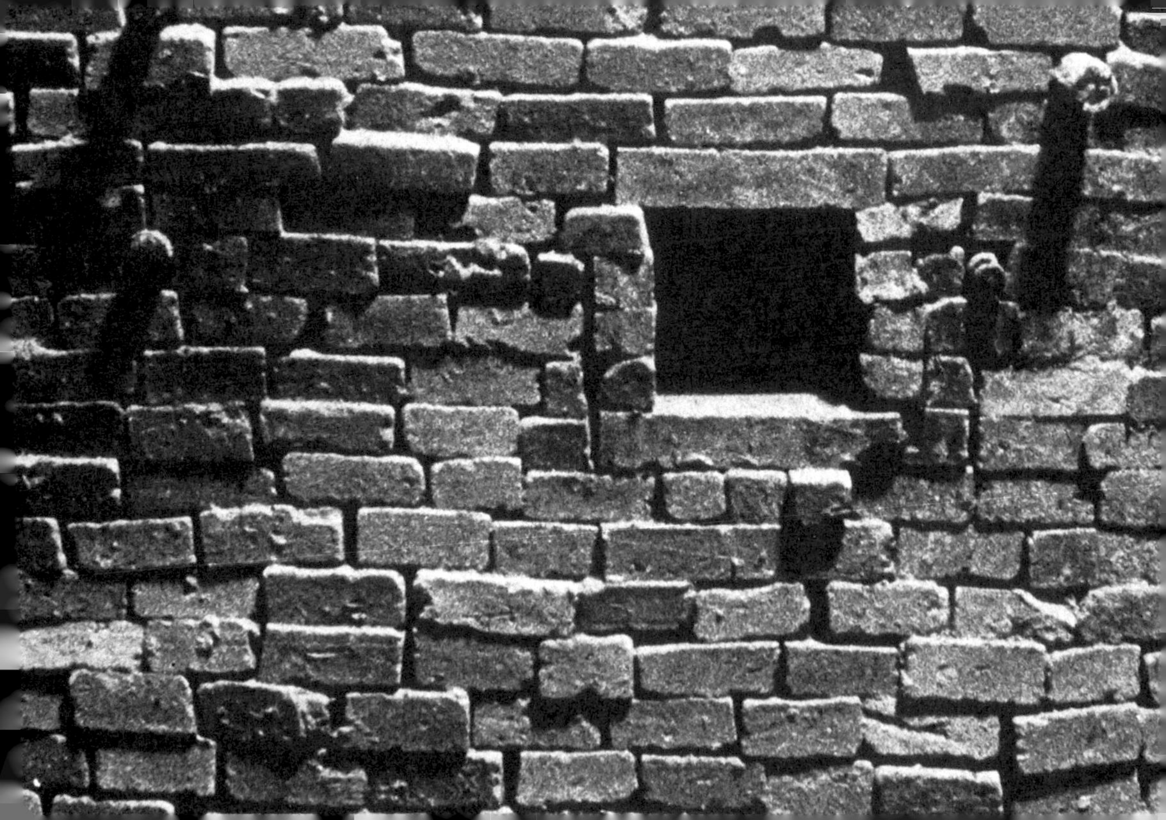

Turds steaming with growth pilled up to build a shelter, bound to a wrinkled navel by cords of rotting grass. In the labyrinth a stately seduction culminating on a mossy mound. In the incinerator less lofty processes. In the mastaba stolid rehabilitation after the dirt is eaten. Where does the cavern fit in? Drooling its waters over the lips of the hills. Last week there was no longer a stream there and other round hills seem to have sprung to camouflage the first two. Is that the cave where the rain was made? When it still rained? Looking up the cliffs from the quarry. Noticing a channel in the wall. When the winter solstice full moon shines here the shadows of the structures below would draw shapes on the slope—shapes not merely reminiscent of the pictographs on the shards.

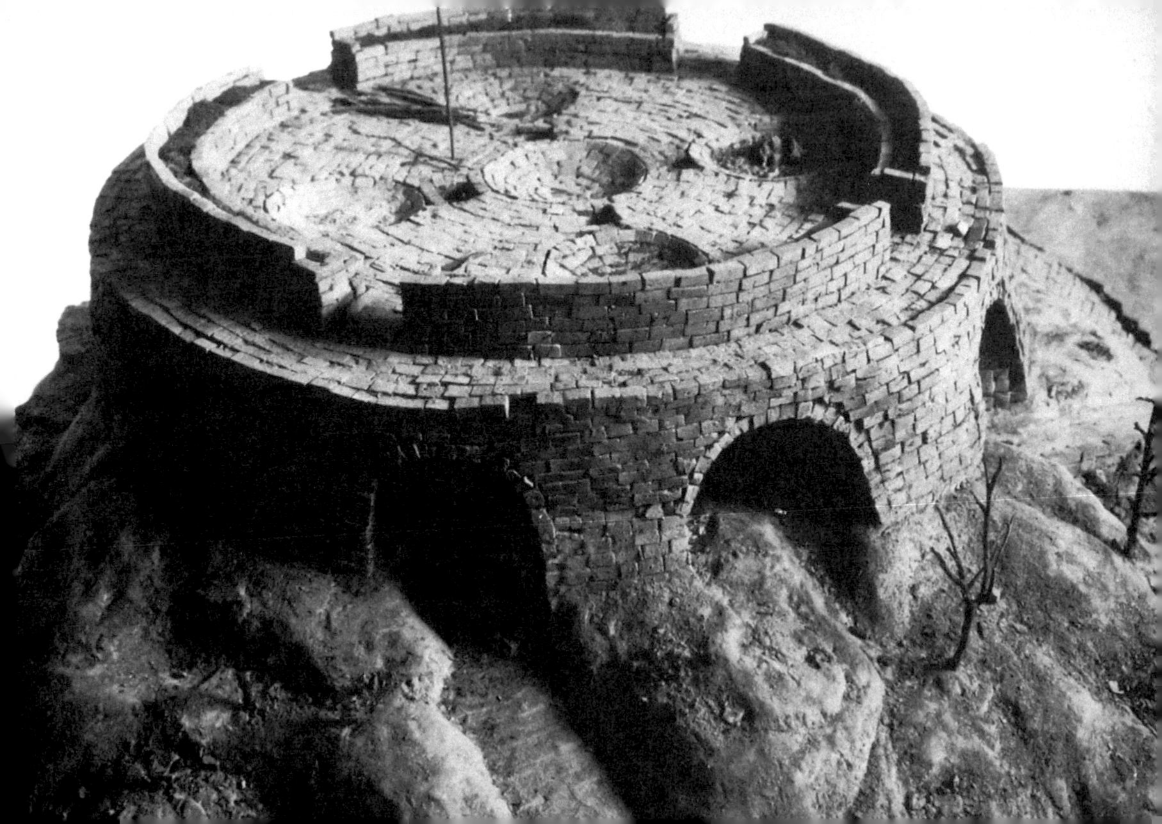

First the doubtful, opaque shards and now the poems or prayers or invocations inside the vessels in the cave—scratched on the concave clay by fingernails functioning as blades. You write to me! You have language, but you seem not to use it the way we do. There is no attempt to lay down laws, to detail events past or present, to build any kind of narrative at all. Where is the time you told me? Are the travellers' paths on the land your only stories? Are your buildings your only laws? Your dwellings your only books? The reinhabited, re-evolved ritual areas your only history? All real, all there. The shards are the letters and the vessels the phrases. Hard little words, like icons, like objects. And then nothing between them and the numbered great design. But I am being carried away, again. Across the ravine and up the mountain. Like everything else here this makes no sense in terms of what we've learned. No wonder X suggests I take a leave. Go back for a week to what he calls civilization and regain my perspective.

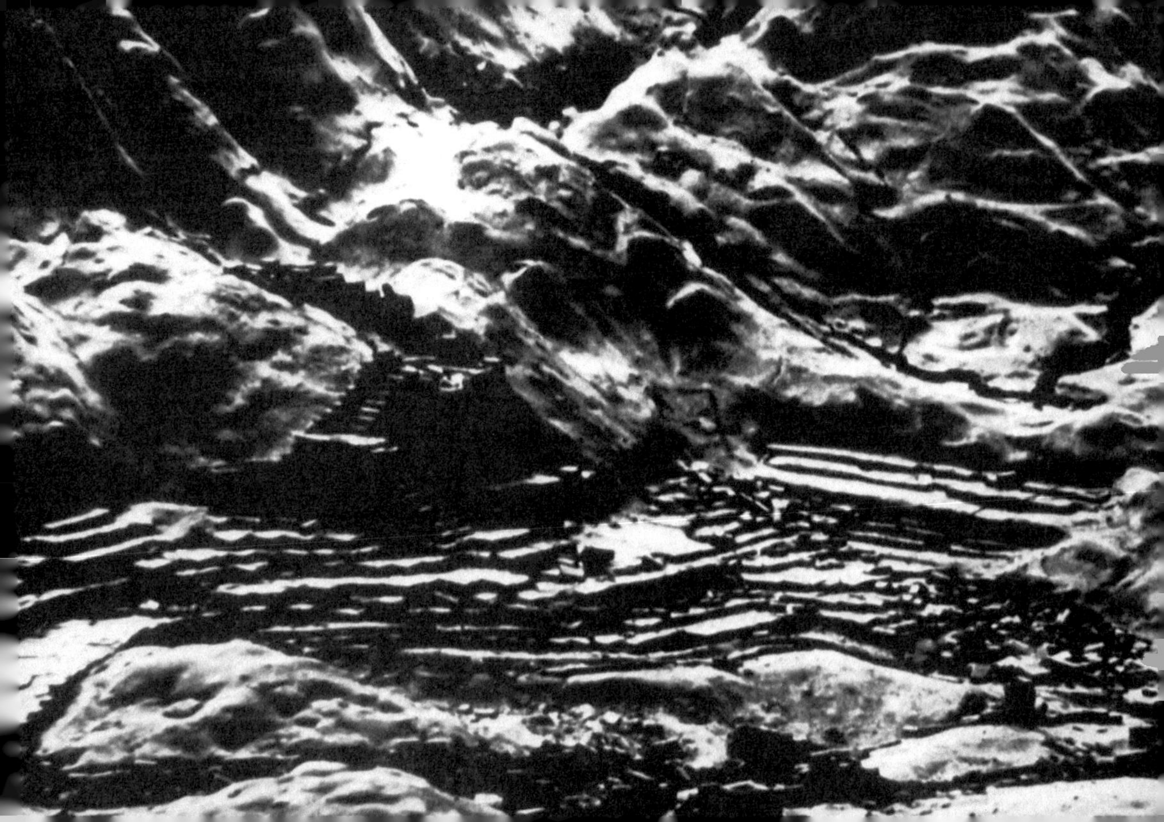

Of course I can't go. You won't let me go. Yet. I am becoming the colors of the land. Pink and yellow and red and gray. I am dreaming a red ritual in which the women very grandly very tenderly smear with their thumbs a dab of menstrual blood on every other woman's forehead. When the men with similar gestures make the same marks on their own brows with red mud. And then join hands in a great ring around the petaled pillar. I am dreaming I try to break out of the ring but find my hands have grown like branches into the hands of the man and woman at my sides. To break the ring will bring disaster. So I stay. In the distance I feel but cannot see a very different pillar. A great gray dour stone with angled sides, vertically striated, sharp edged, towering over the open-mouthed mountain like a column of smoke or a tornado.

Those without arms will raise the waters.

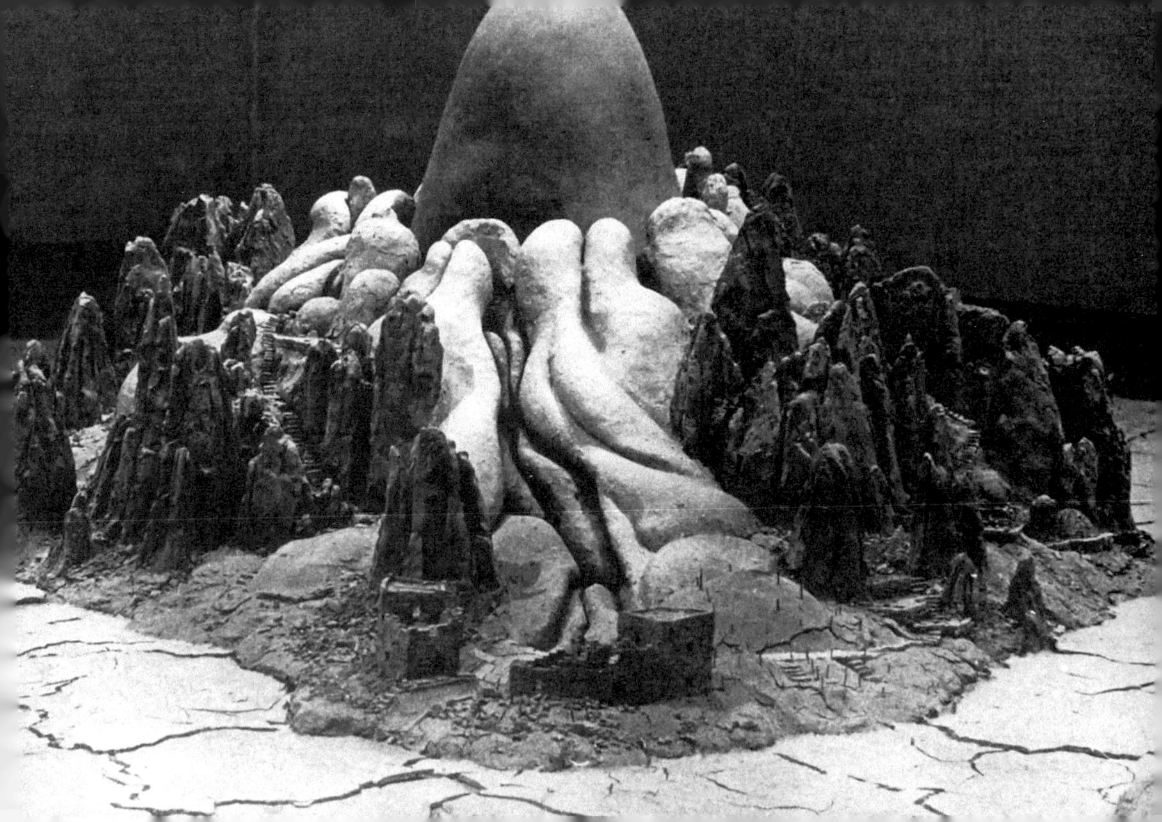

You sucked the stone from my belly and wear it behind your ear. Blue, pale, with black and green veins like a map across it. We fondle our stone in the darkness. It glows like the butterflies' wings. We remember the water and the music. You can't tell me where they went. We made love as is your custom in one of the sacred places of the earth reserved for anger, pleasure, tears and moans. Afterwards we built together the prescribed forms. I the male one, you the female one—with which your people commemorate all union.

October 31: You tell me to open the cage, to release the prisoners below me.

November 1: X reports he saw a Trail Snake disappearing into the foundations of the road-dwelling today. He is almost elated. He claims they have been here all along, though the Trail Snake (unmistakable, he says, its blood-red and grain-gold diamonds) is not native to these parts. With his usual logic he has resolved this problem too; it was imported, long ago, perhaps in a trader's basket, and its hibernation habits are different here, which

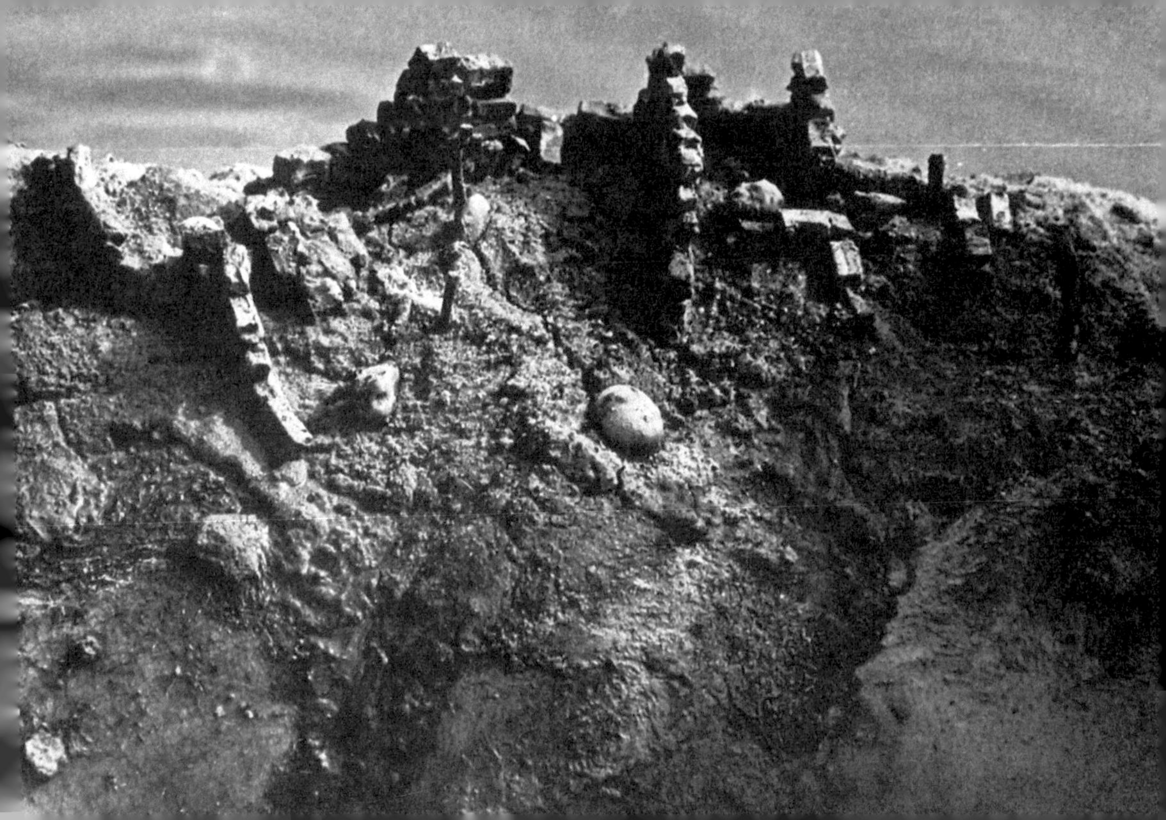

accounts for our having seen no reptiles all this time. Tomorrow, still more excited, he will report an iguana near the circular city. This will be harder to explain and he will think perhaps it was a mirage. He will laugh nervously and hope my "fevered imagination" is not contagious.

What if one clock falls behind? It's only natural. Meeting another half way. Yes, waiting. I hold two photographs of myself side by side. In one I am thirty-five years old, in the other ten. To try and understand.

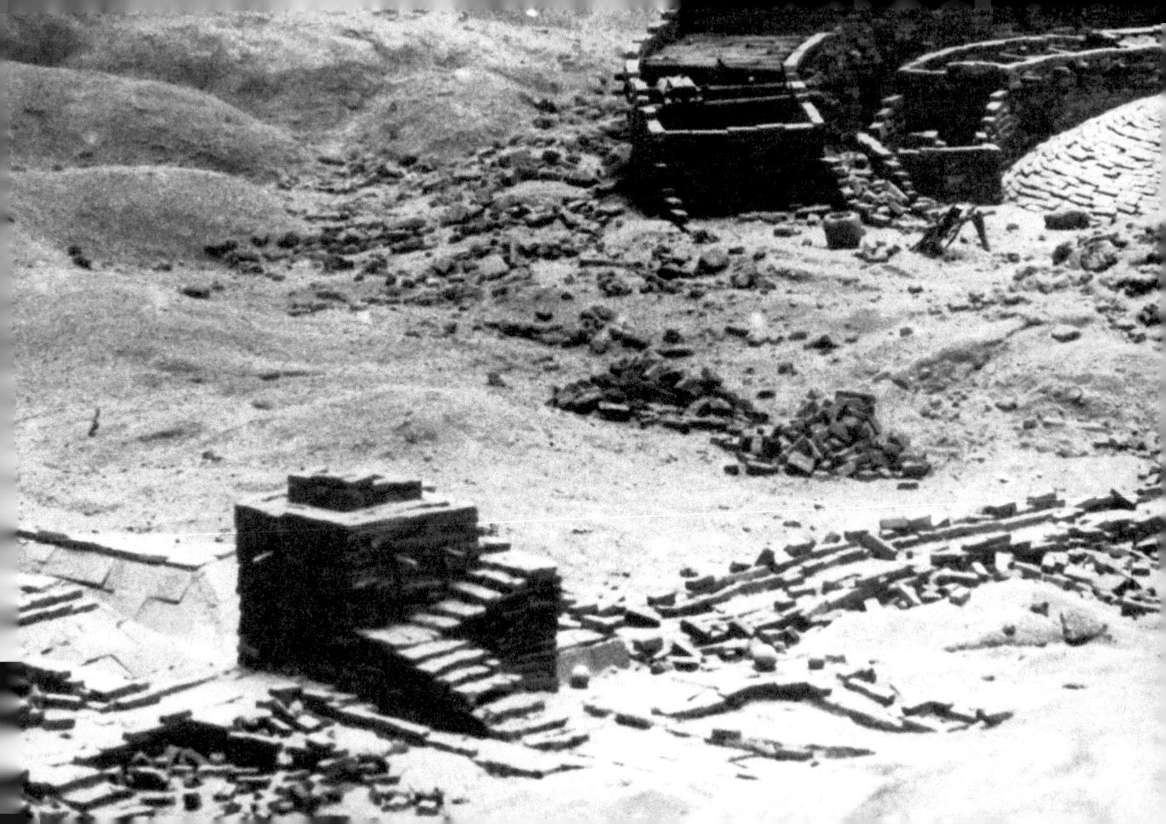

You found yourselves in a strange city magnified to catastrophic scale, booming and blaring down on you. A gray city already in ruin but still inhabited, still being built. A city where some are struggling to eat, and others are eating them. Huge bodies filled the canyons and you hid in your homes from their eyes. Some never saw you. Others came and walked your paths. Some were afraid and you turned to dust before their eyes. You submitted to curious caresses, meteors, casual deaths. You heard them talk of places inaccessible but not yet ruins where the Eaters, the Unsharers, gorged themselves and clung to the illusion of possessing the earth. When the spirals crumbled you saw them re-erected and crumbled again. You were invisible to those whose eyes looked only out and up and down, to those floating precariously on power or sunk too deeply in despair. But some became adept at following your distances and entered, dreamed this place.

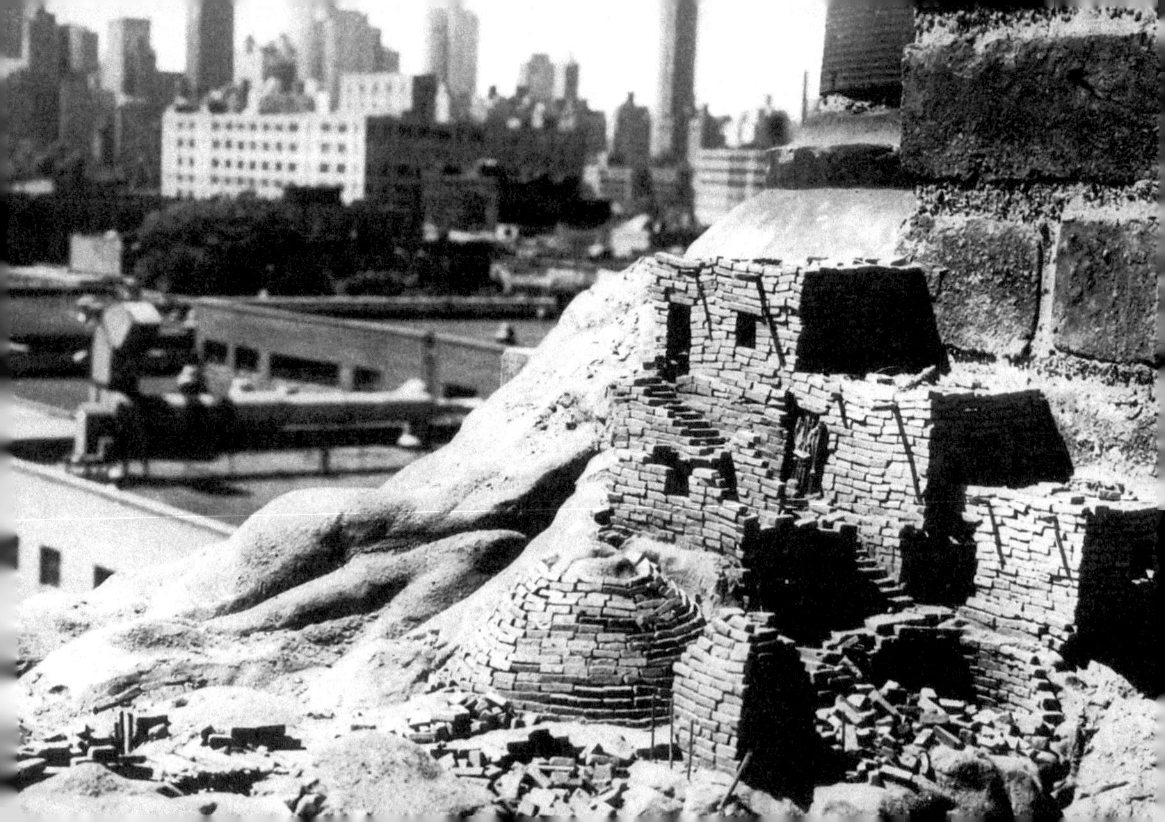

When was the best time? Before the patterns were revealed? Before the connections were made? When the fires burned in clear straight paths and stars lined up over the waters in the earth? You move away from me. You fear divisions— good and evil, fact and dream, now and then, large and small, better and worse.

Are you growing or rotting? Do you measure time in nights or days? Years by moon or sun? You whisper both. You say I mustn't choose.

November 14: The linguists' reports on the shards baffle X. I try to hide my triumph. They are names, all names, but from innumerable different languages, and dialects from wildly varying times and places—some earlier, some later than the carbon dates we're going on. How can that be? It can be because this place is everywhere and all time. X thinks archeology concerns only the past. He thinks the people are dead. He doesn't see the childhoods surrounding us like sand not yet rock. I am watching for the fossils turned inside out, my own imprint in the land.

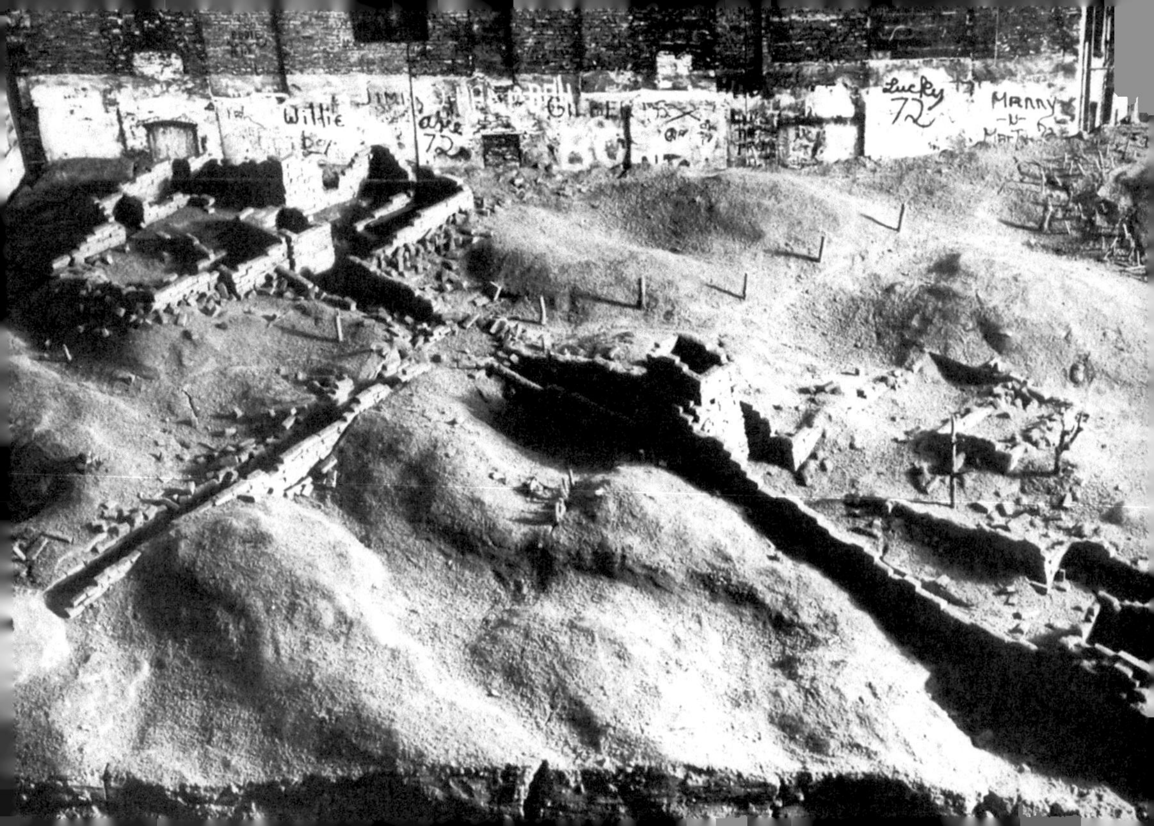
Willie boy
Lucky
72

If the lizard bites the butterfly the cave swallows the serpent.

Are you a man or a woman? A woman or a man? Sometimes I think I feel you entering me. Sometimes my tumescences have entered you. Sometimes we are all tongues. Sometimes you are all lips and orifices, and sometimes rolling smooth and solid surfaces. And what am *I*, then?

I dreamed I was your father. I dreamed I was a child. I dreamed I tripped over a mountain. I dreamed I lived in a wasps' nest. I dreamed you were curled up inside of me. I dreamed I was curled up inside of you. I dreamed I gave birth to a yellow snail, to a litter of idols, to the sea. I dreamed a great foot was descending on me but I turned myself into the earth and we made love instead. I dreamed that I built a house from grains of sand, that I was battling my way through a field of clover in the midst of November gales, that you and I drank from a well of blood, that we played ball with a seed pearl and batted it with the trunk of a redwood tree. I dreamed the world shrank and expanded and there was no such thing as size. I dreamed a little figure

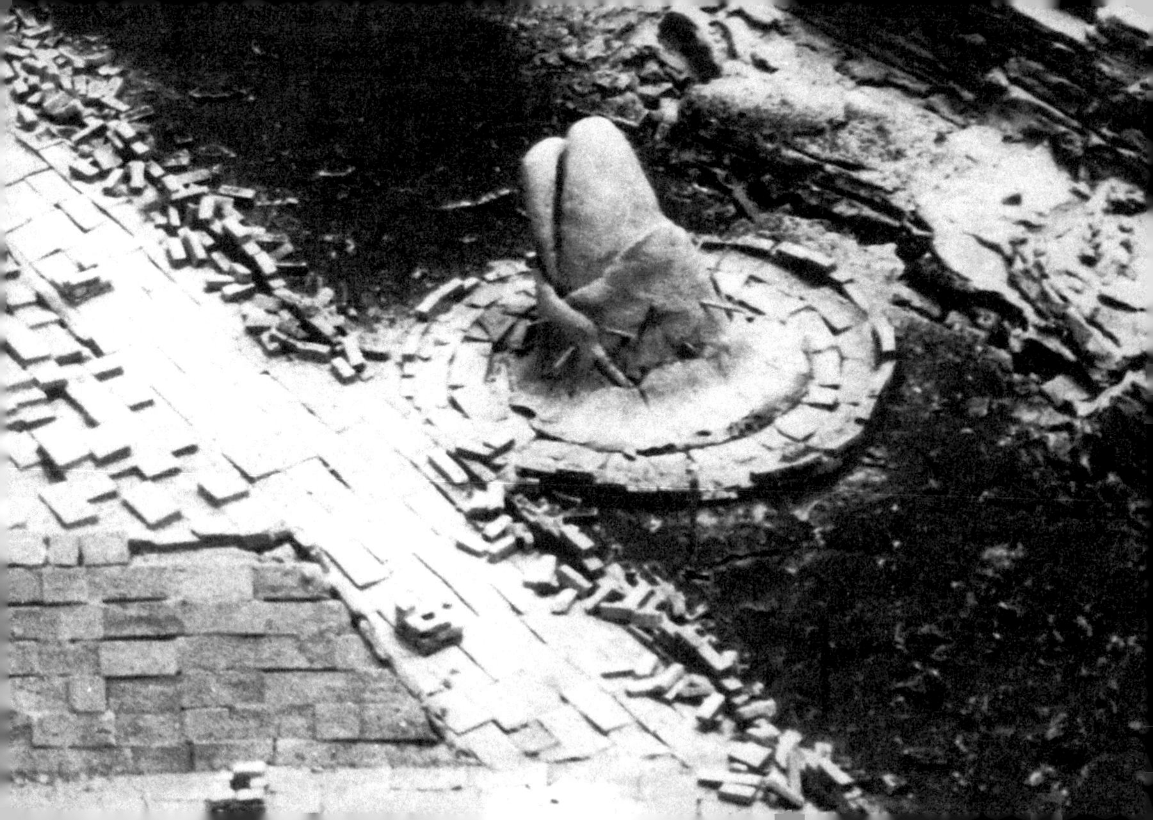

running down a long road. A red road, dusty, vague. Behind him waits the mother. Great distances are put between her and her child, who doesn't know the forbidden road is circular and inescapable.
It must be winter. The days are short, thin and pale as a bone in the black chamber.

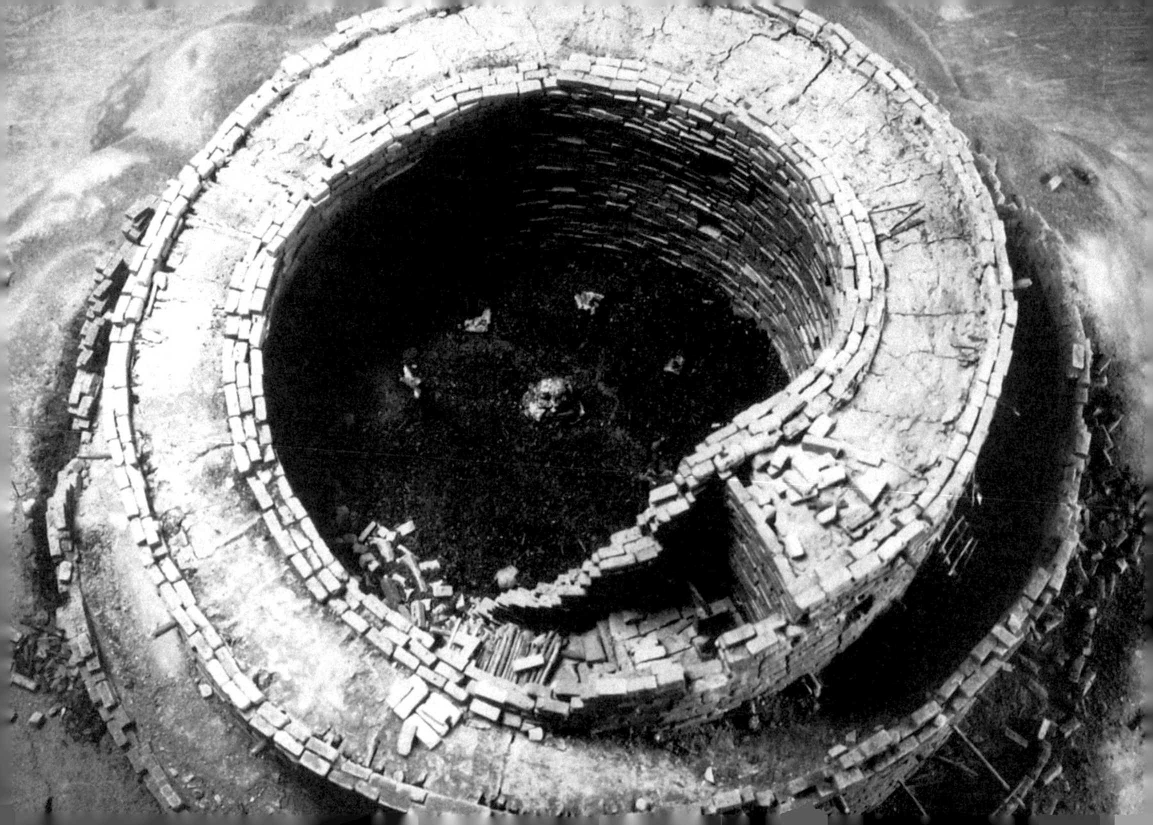

December 4: For weeks now nothing new has been found and we have resorted to the tedious and exhausting task of cataloguing the bones on the great skeleton. X is depressed by the subversive aspect of simplicity and repetition. The stubbornness of the cycle. The oblivion of the horizon. But you drum insistently inside me and the longer the nights the better. You tell me your house consumed you at one season and at another you consumed your house.
Nature is my slave, says X. I shudder.
So resurrection will be rebellion. Chaos re-emerging to be unmolded, this time. To float, change, reform, transform—a moving target too fast for the glass slivers and book covers. Is that what you're trying to tell me?

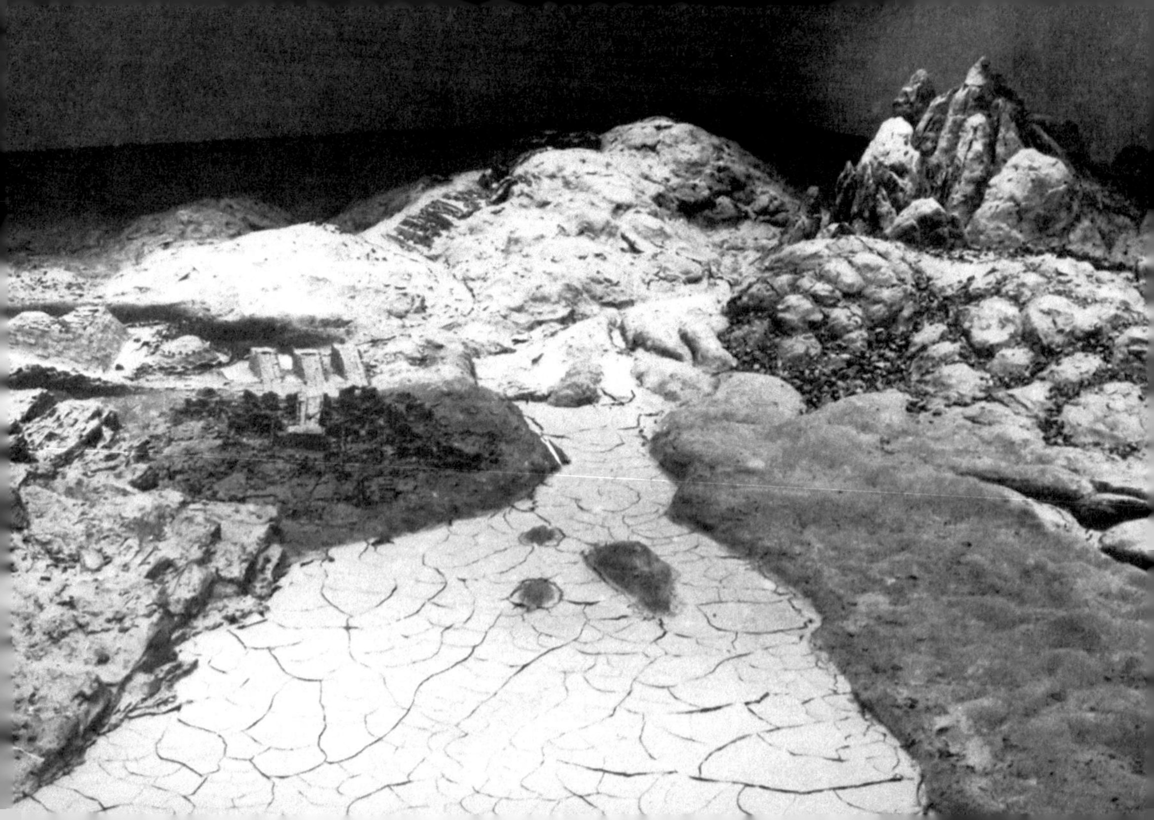

I dreamed a world rising and falling into a whole. I dreamed that world in turn broke up and was set afloat on a vast sea to seek its next form. I dreamed a protozoic prose, amoebic amnesia, a cannibal's chronicle. I dreamed it into fragments again. I reformed it and made of it a very different place. Inside out. I dreamed this line of generations also abandoned and what came afterwards is what we see. From one time to the next the fires burned and swallowed and returned the round soft building blocks; equally the hard ones falling into sharp bright angles.

December 21: In the rings of ashes that lie beneath the cairns we found a series of small round stones, each with a different pattern like the stone behind your ear and the two stones between your legs and the stone pillar in my cave.

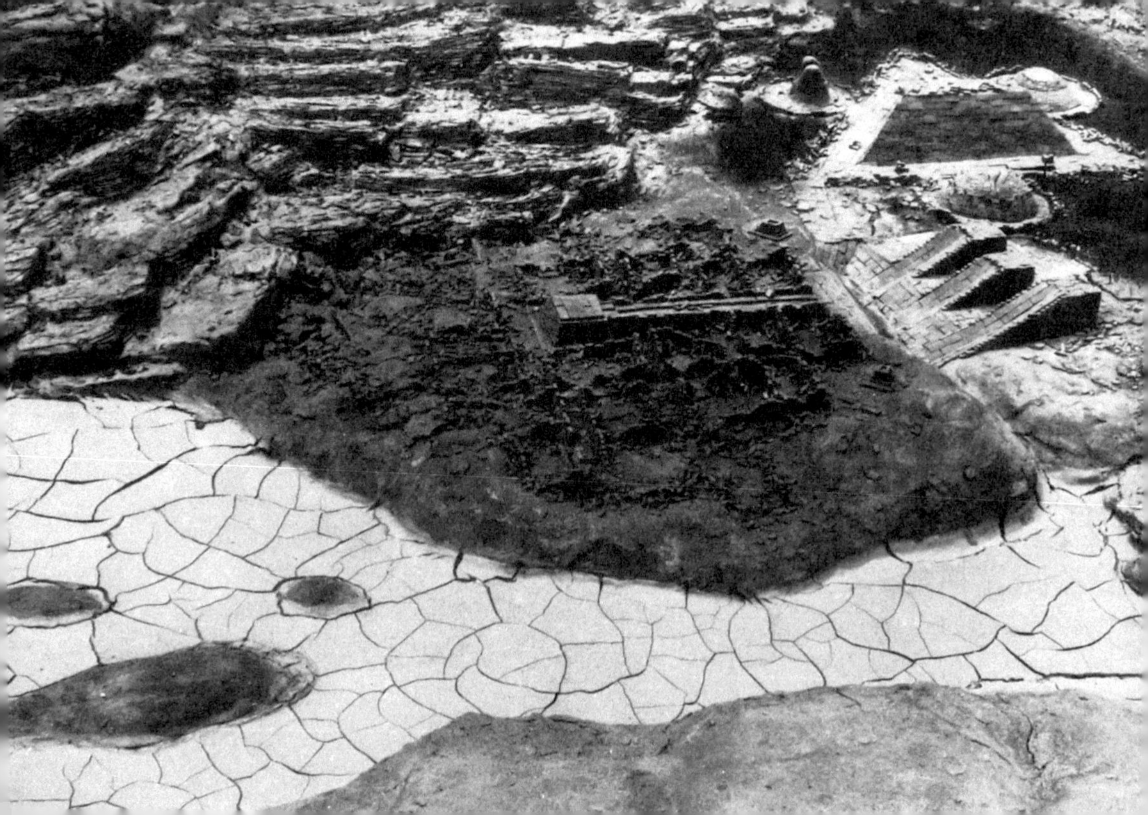

Red earth, substance revealed, green furry skin torn off. Sometimes you guard her with red brick armor, bristling spines, cruel stakes.
We put our stones back in the fire. A flaming wheel rolls down the mountain and explodes into the lake. Tatters of flesh and skin remain on pointed sticks. Offered to the petaled tower. Now even I turn away. From which direction did the violence come?
In this forest of leafless trees, on this limpid knoll, near that sagging mound with scales of brick ... First I bit your thumb off then a chunk of shoulder. Your round eyes I swallowed whole and tears and bile and blood ran down my chin. Your mouth on my breast was sucking, biting, baring flesh while I spat out the hairs and gulped your sperm. I found I was bellyless, gutless, lost in your channels and you in mine.

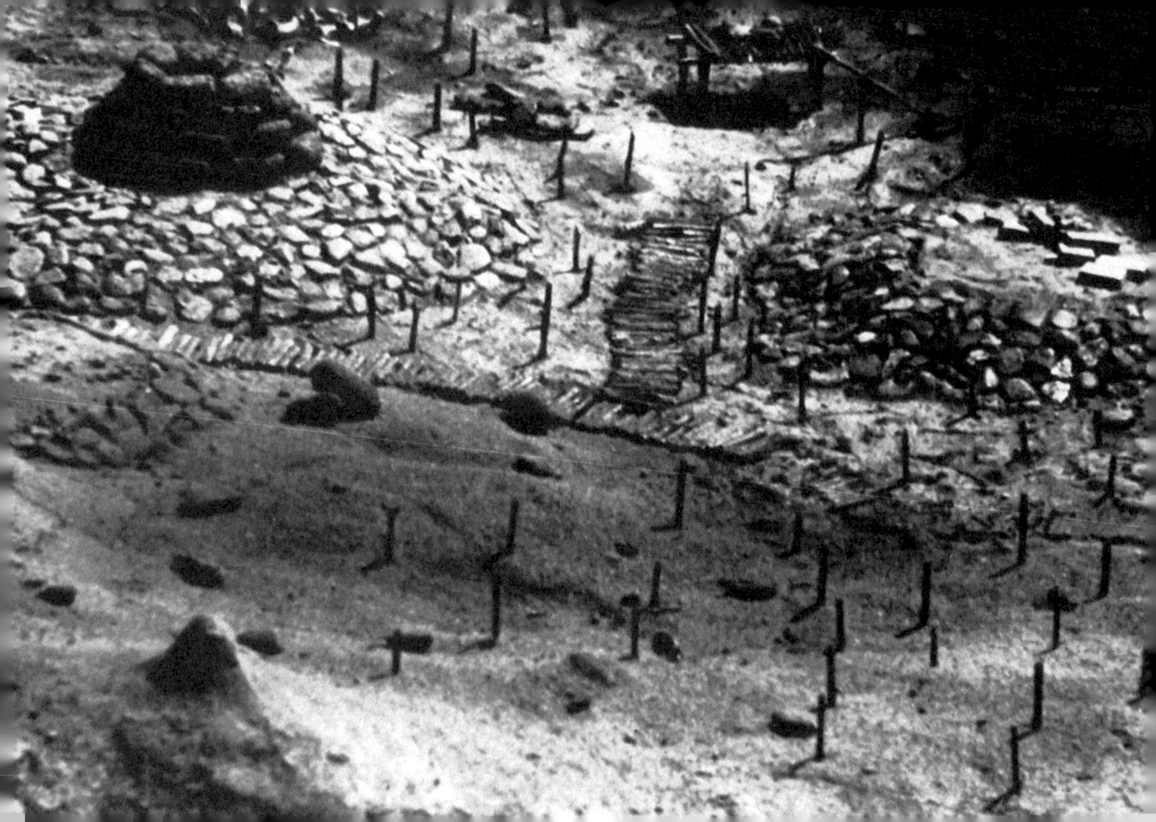

In memory of trees. In memory of water. In memory of music. In memory of growth.

The wind is blowing on top of the mountain. The lips of its summit are sometimes visible from the slopes below where we wait, and sometimes veiled by a pinkish cloud of dust and mist combined. On the north side plump curves give way to cliffs sliced to gray quarried walls. We look up in anticipation. It is about to begin. A flock of white birds, foreigners, fly over the crest, their underbellies pink from the reflected earth, and the people murmur that this is a good omen.

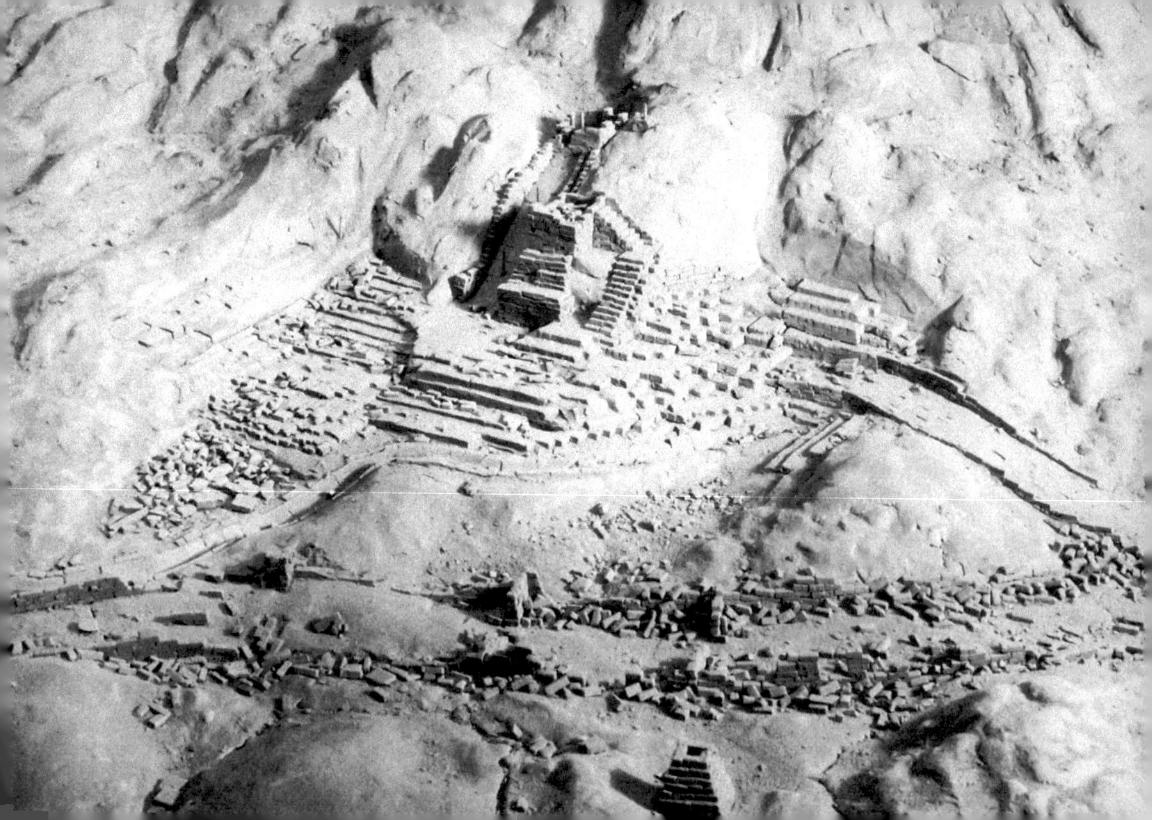

We move as a body, the parts interchangeable. We have been a breast, soft and taut and layered. We have been a thigh, hugging bone and muscle. We have been an eye, doubling as a womb. We have been an arm, flung wide in embrace. We have been a penis, throbbing in expectation. We have been a belly, empty, full and empty again. We have been a finger, touching our skin. We have been a mind, thinking the thoughts that begin the process.

Do you remember? Just in time. February. When we were seeds in the dark dome. When we were grains of rock in the bricks that covered the chamber. When we were the two parts coming together. When the wind blew under the earth.

In the morning the land is created—soft and wet and sloping. By midday the crops are planted. The village flourishes in the afternoon. By dusk layers of dust are settling on forgotten walls. And in the night the cataclysm opens its legs to a new season.

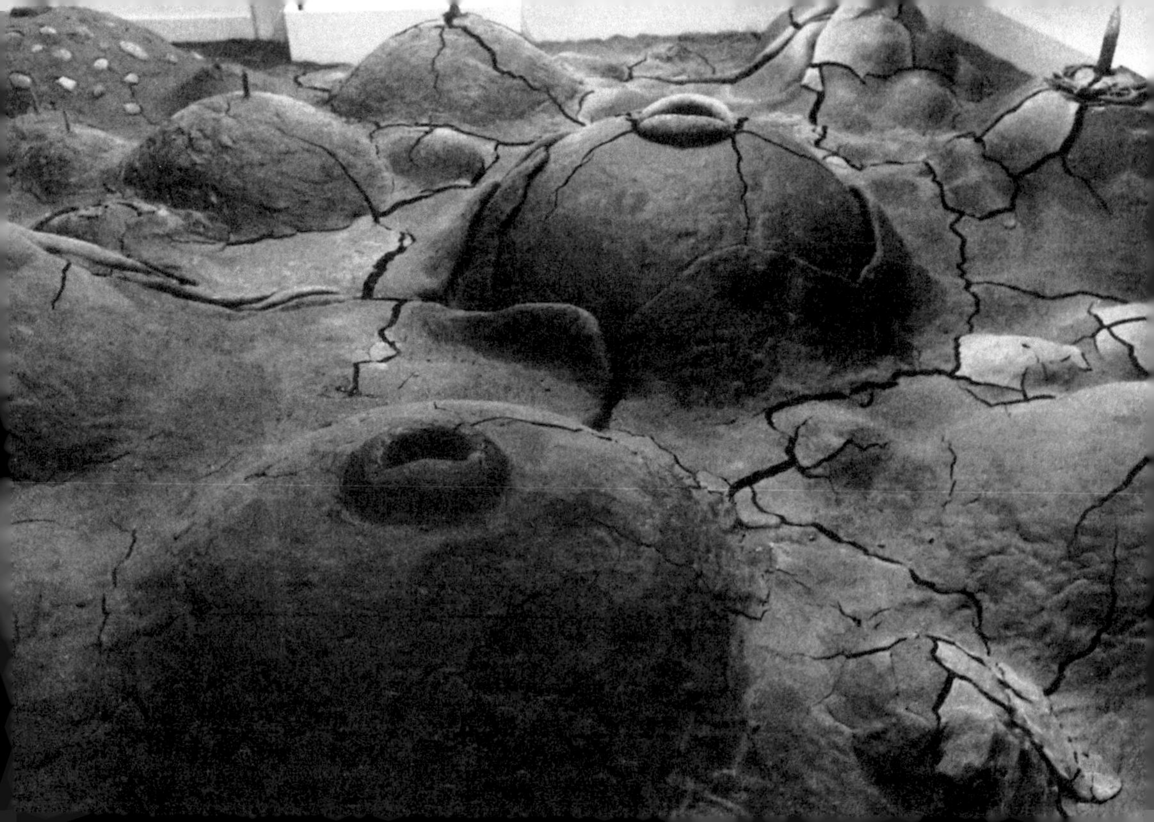

They will look for meaning, which they have separated from meaning. I see what you mean, they will cry without seeing. They will say I, and you, because they don't remember.

It must be spring again. The seeds I have eaten are eating their way out of me. The waters are bursting through the hole I have dug. The elusive cavern in the mountain waits. We will wait too. Since we found no artifacts in the ancient caves, X thinks we'll find none here. It can be my last question, he teases. And the safety of the entrance must be tested first. The glimpse we had, though. You beckon me to join you there. You don't believe in oblivion.

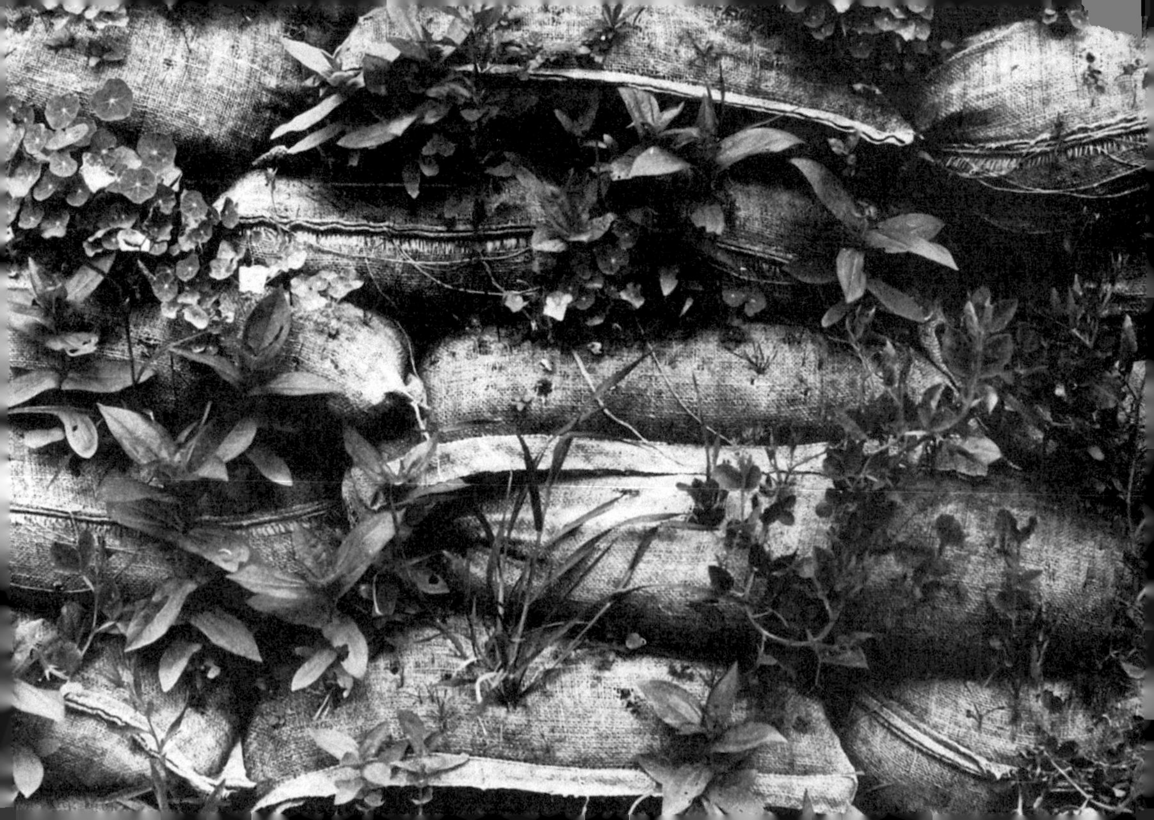

I had gone as far as the dried up stream bed between the two round hills so like the other rounded hills around them. Turned to face the entrance and saw instead ...
How can a snake make love with a butterfly?
How can a butterfly open her wings and expose her softest parts? Only when flying, then. A soaring descent. When the rain came down for the first time since the people left.

April 14: A peculiarly ecstatic death. Who would have suspected that network of underground streams, that dark subterranean pool? No wonder the roof fell in. No wonder she lost her way. No wonder she won her mind. Why was she digging so deep?